engage

Level 2

Teacher's Book

Nicholas Tims

Gregory J. Manin   Alicia Artusi

OXFORD
UNIVERSITY PRESS

OXFORD
UNIVERSITY PRESS

Great Clarendon Street, Oxford OX2 6DP

Oxford University Press is a department of the University of Oxford.
It furthers the University's objective of excellence in research, scholarship,
and education by publishing worldwide in

Oxford New York

Auckland Cape Town Dar es Salaam Hong Kong Karachi
Kuala Lumpur Madrid Melbourne Mexico City Nairobi
New Delhi Shanghai Taipei Toronto

With offices in

Argentina Austria Brazil Chile Czech Republic France Greece
Guatemala Hungary Italy Japan Poland Portugal Singapore
South Korea Switzerland Thailand Turkey Ukraine Vietnam

OXFORD and OXFORD ENGLISH are registered trade marks of
Oxford University Press in the UK and in certain other countries

First published 2008

2011 2010 2009 2008
10 9 8 7 6 5 4 3 2 1

ISBN: 978 0 19 453656 1

Printed in China

Contents

Introduction

Overview of *Engage*	iv
Using the Student Book	vi
Other components	ix
CD track listings	xi

Teaching notes

Student Book contents		2
Remember		4
Unit 1	Our world	9
Review 1		16
Unit 2	All about me	17
Review 2		24
Unit 3	Different styles	25
Review 3		32
Unit 4	On vacation	33
Review 4		40
Unit 5	Music world	41
Review 5		48
Unit 6	The coolest places	49
Review 6		56
Unit 7	Crime scene	57
Review 7		64
Unit 8	Survivors	65
Review 8		72
Unit 9	The sporting life	73
Review 9		80
Unit 10	The future	81
Review 10		88
Unit 11	Plans	89
Review 11		96
Unit 12	Life experiences	97
Review 12		103

Workbook answer key

Workbook units 1–12	104

Introduction

Overview of *Engage*

Engage uses a wide range of topics to contextualize new language, combining a strong visual impact with an exceptionally clear, well-paced syllabus.

Engage is easy for both teachers and students to use. It is stimulating but not confusing; structured but not rigid; straightforward without being simplistic.

The material encourages students to truly **engage** with the process of learning English at every level.

Topics

By focusing on a different topic in each teaching unit, students use English to **engage** with the world around them. Sometimes this is through factual presentations, sometimes through fictional characters and situations – but always with the aim of teaching students about a particular aspect of the real world. A wide range of topics and formats are used, mixing cultural and cross-curricular features with more light-hearted presentations.

Vocabulary

In **Engage**, vocabulary provides the gateway to the unit topic. Each teaching unit presents two sets of active vocabulary, using a mixture of textual and visual input. Together, the topic and vocabulary set give students the tools they will need for subsequent grammar practice, and for skills work at the end of the unit. All the items are modeled on the *Audio CDs* for students to listen and repeat as a class.

Additional vocabulary input is provided by the *Workbook*, where **Extend your vocabulary** exercises introduce a further set of words related to the topic of the relevant Student Book lesson.

Grammar

Engage features two single-page grammar lessons per unit. Each lesson presents and practices a single small point, rather than dabbling in several points at a time. Tenses and other complex areas of grammar are divided over a number of lessons and units. This focused, step-by-step approach makes new language more accessible and easier to digest.

Comprehensive grammar charts are given on the page, so that students have a correct model to work from at all times. Grammar practice activities are carefully graded, from recognition exercises at the start of the lesson, to sentence production at the end, with the result that students can see real progress as they work their way through the lesson.

Communication

Each grammar lesson ends with a short **Over to you!** activity, which provides the opportunity for meaningful, personalized practice in the form of a simple speaking activity. A guided preparatory stage, usually written, builds students' confidence before they speak. All **Over to you!** activities can be done either as a whole class or, if conditions allow, in pairs.

Skills

Special attention is given to the gradual, controlled development of the four skills, through a two-page **Living English** section at the end of every unit. Reading features in every unit, along with two of the remaining three skills.

From the very first unit, **Engage** aims to build students' competence in both receptive and productive skills. Simple strategies help students learn how to read and write more effectively, while speaking lessons include guided exercises on pronunciation within the context of short dialogs. For both speaking and writing, a brief, carefully structured model is provided on the page, so that students have a clear framework on which to hang their own ideas. Listening scripts and activities are deliberately short and simple to begin with, in order to help students gradually get used to recognizing the sounds of spoken English. Levels 2 and 3 build on this by introducing a series of basic listening strategies.

Learning

It is important that students learn to take control of their learning and study techniques from the earliest opportunity. **Engage** addresses this need by including study skills as part of the **Review** lessons. These cover a range of issues—from the basics of understanding instructions in the coursebook, to ways of using English outside the classroom—and always include a follow-up practice activity.

Mixed ability

The flexibility of **Engage** makes it ideal for mixed-ability classes. An example of this is the series of vocabulary and grammar-related puzzles in the **Magazine** section of the Student Book, to which fast finishers are directed at the end of each grammar lesson. The core material itself is also easy to adapt to the needs of different groups or individuals, allowing the teacher to place more or less emphasis on listening, speaking, reading or writing as appropriate.

Photocopiable *Mixed-Ability Worksheets* are designed to cater for students at different stages of learning, with both support activities for weaker students, and freer extension activities for the more able students. Further suggestions for graded follow-up activities are given in the *Teacher's Book*.

Cross-curricular content

A strong emphasis on real-world topics provides an excellent springboard for dealing with other areas of the curriculum. Throughout **Engage**, students are encouraged not just to learn a series of words and structures, but rather to use English as a tool for expanding their knowledge of the world around them. Features on music, movies and popular culture sit comfortably alongside texts about geography, history and technology. Whatever the topic, the aim is to make it informative, accessible and relevant.

In addition, the material gives numerous opportunities for reinforcing basic values and areas of general education. For instance, the importance of tolerance and respect for others is a theme which runs throughout each book, as demonstrated by the inclusion of a diverse range of nationalities, cultures and social backgrounds in the presentations and reading texts. Other areas seen in **Engage** include gender equality, consumer education, and health.

The **Unit summaries** in this *Teacher's Book* list all relevant values and cross-curricular subjects covered in each unit.

Extension

Engage features a wealth of extra resources, which can be used with the whole class, as extra self-study material, or as extension for individual students. Within the Student Book, the **Magazine** section provides puzzles, extra reading texts, and guided projects.

The *Workbook* includes two **Extend your vocabulary** exercises per unit; also featured in the Workbook are four **Extra reading** lessons, based on extracts from the *Oxford Bookworms Library*.

The *Teacher's Book* includes suggestions for extra follow-up activities where appropriate.

The photocopiable *Mixed-Ability Worksheets* each include one freer extension exercise for more able students, as well as extra support for weaker students and a practice activity for the rest of the class.

Recycling

In each level of **Engage** the early units review and consolidate the principal areas of grammar from the previous level. Familiar vocabulary and grammar is periodically revisited and extended throughout the book, so that students are always building on what they know.

New language is constantly recycled at each stage of the course. Each new vocabulary set is immediately practiced, and then actively used in subsequent grammar lessons and skills lessons. All vocabulary sets and grammar points are systematically reviewed in **Review** lessons. In addition, the last teaching unit of each *Student Book* ends with a game which reviews all the structures covered in the book.

An additional resource for reviewing recently acquired language is through the **Project** pages of the **Magazine** section. The projects have been carefully designed so that students review and actively use the most important language from the previous three units.

Further practice is provided in the *Workbook* and *Mixed-Ability Worksheets*.

Assessment

Photocopiable *Tests* provide a convenient method of assessment for both teacher and students. There is one two-page test covering vocabulary, grammar and reading, for use after every *Student Book* unit. Exercises are graded in such a way that all abilities of students are catered for.

Using the Student Book

Teaching units are divided as follows: the units start with a single page of **Introducing the topic**. This introduces vocabulary related to the topic of the unit, and is followed by three sections of two pages each: **Exploring the topic**, **Building the topic** and **Living English**. **Exploring the topic** and **Building the topic** each have one page of grammar. **Exploring the topic** also has one page of reading while **Building the topic** contains vocabulary presentation and practice. These are followed by **Living English** with two pages of skills work. The unit ends with a single page **Review** section. All the material is organized so that one page represents one lesson and teaches one point.

Introducing the topic

Vocabulary

Introducing the topic opens each unit. This page is an illustrated presentation of vocabulary related to the unit topic. In most cases, activities involve some form of labeling or matching of words to visuals, sometimes requiring students to choose the correct word to complete a caption. The answers are always recorded on the **Audio CDs**, allowing students to hear the new words, either alone or in short phrases, and to practice saying them as they repeat.

> You may wish to play the recording twice at this point—once for students to check their answers, then a second time for them to listen and repeat. Alternatively, you could model the words yourself.

Following the vocabulary presentation, a **Recycling** exercise encourages students to use previously learned vocabulary which is in some way related to the new lexical set.

Exploring the topic

Reading

This double page section starts with a reading text. Although the text includes a new grammar structure, students are not expected to actively use the new grammar on this page.

> At some point during the lesson, students have the opportunity to listen to the complete text as recorded on the **Audio CDs**, at the same time as they read the text on the page. This has the advantage of exposing students to the sounds of a new grammar structure before they come to study it in the next lesson. Reading and listening at the same time also familiarizes students with the relationship between the written and spoken word in English, and gives them extra listening practice.

Grammar

The right-hand page of **Exploring the topic** formally presents the new grammar structure first seen in the text on the previous page. The headings on the page describe the new language in both structural and functional terms. A more detailed explanation of usage is given in the **Grammar Summary** at the end of the **Student Book**, and you may wish to draw students' attention to this during the lesson.

Form is modeled using a comprehensive chart, which features sentences taken or adapted from the previous page where possible. The advantage of having a completed chart on the page is that students always have a correct reference point to help them.

Sometimes a **Take note!** box appears after the grammar chart. This draws attention to a particular grammatical detail—such as a spelling rule—which students will need in order to correctly produce the target language.

> Once students have looked at the grammar chart in the book, it can sometimes be a good idea to get them involved in filling in an "alternative" chart on the chalk board, using different example sentences. This provides you with an opportunity to clear up any difficulties with either form or meaning, using the students' mother tongue if appropriate. It also serves to highlight common mistakes.

Grammar practice is generally provided in the form of three graded exercises, followed by an **Over to you!** activity. The exercises begin with simple recognition, for example matching or choosing the correct answer. The aim is to get students accustomed to seeing and identifying the new structure, before moving on to production at the level of individual words and verb forms, and phrase and sentence-level production in the final grammar exercise.

At this point in the lesson, a **Finished?** symbol directs fast finishers to the **Magazine** section at the back of the book. Here they will find a word puzzle, brainteaser, or other fun activity which uses the vocabulary and grammar from **Exploring the topic**. You can, of course, use the puzzle as a fun activity for the whole class. Answers to all the **Magazine** activities are given within the teaching notes for the corresponding lesson.

At the end of the **Grammar** lesson, **Over to you!** gives students the opportunity to personalize the new language and exchange information in a meaningful way. A written preparatory stage builds students' confidence by ensuring that they have had time to plan what they are going to say.

All **Over to you!** activities have been designed so that they can be successfully completed either as teacher-led exchanges in open class, or alternatively in pairs and groups.

Building the topic

Vocabulary

In **Building the topic**, the **Vocabulary** page introduces a different perspective on the unit topic, and presents a new set of words, which are taught, modeled and practiced.

Grammar

The new language presented in the **Grammar** lesson is usually related in some way to the previous grammar point, for example presenting the negative or question forms of a new tense. Sometimes, a conscious decision has been made to deal with something relatively lightweight in **Building the topic**, especially in cases where **Exploring the topic** has covered a more demanding area of grammar.

Living English

These two pages deal specifically with skills work. The left-hand page always features a reading text and related activities, while the right-hand page covers two of the remaining three skills. We recognize that different school systems and classroom conditions require teachers to place more or less emphasis on certain skills. By dealing with each skill as a separate lesson, this section of the unit gives you the flexibility to choose the material which best suits your own requirements.

Reading

Skills reading texts in **Living English** are longer than in the previous two sections of the unit. They deal with an aspect of the unit topic, with a factual focus where possible, and actively use the vocabulary and grammar of the unit. Any new vocabulary—whilst kept to a minimum—is included in the **Word list** at the end of the *Student Book*, and the language structures are strictly limited to what students have seen so far.

The accompanying exercises are designed to gradually build up students' reading comprehension skills. The first exercise focuses on global comprehension, while the second requires a more detailed understanding of the text.

Approximately half of the **Reading** lessons include **Reading skills** boxes, around which the comprehension activities are based. These boxes help students to acquire and practice simple but important strategies from the very first unit onwards.

In order to help students remember reading strategies, it is a good idea to review them from time to time. For example, if they have recently looked at how to use photos to predict the content of a text, it is worth encouraging students to do this whenever possible with subsequent reading texts.

All reading texts are recorded on the **Audio CDs**, for additional listening practice.

Listening

Listening scripts usually follow on from the topic of the reading text, and once again the emphasis is on building students' confidence through gradual exposure. There is an initial context check question, followed by more detailed comprehension questions. Scripts are short, and tasks are generally limited to recognition only, especially in the lower levels of the course, so that students are not having to decode several levels of information and write answers all at the same time. In Levels 2 and 3 of **Engage, Listening skills** boxes introduce students to some basic strategies to help with aural comprehension of slightly longer listening passages.

When doing detailed listening activities with the class, it is good practice for students to listen to the recording at least three times. Before playing the recording, give your students time to read the comprehension questions through so that they can predict the information, vocabulary and structures they are going to hear. On the first listening, encourage them not to write anything down, but simply to listen and try to get a general idea. After they have listened, give them a few minutes to try and answer as many questions as they can from memory.

On the second listening, students can check and complete their answers. If necessary, repeat this stage. The third time around, students correct their answers. You may wish to pause the CD at relevant points during the recording so that students can see exactly where the answers are given.

All scripts are recorded on the **Audio CDs**, and reproduced in the teaching notes if not in the *Student Book*.

Writing

Writing lessons are based around a model text, which is carefully structured in such a way that students can follow it exactly when they produce their own compositions. A chart helps students to analyze the model and note down the important information. As a result, they are able to see which parts of the model text can be changed, before thinking of their own ideas. At this point, most students will be ready to write.

> For weaker groups, it might be helpful to go through the model text together and ask students to identify exactly which words and phrases they can change to produce their own piece of writing. If necessary, write the model on the chalk board with the relevant words gapped out, so that students can write it down in their notebooks and then complete it.

In approximately half of the teaching units, the **Writing** lesson includes a simple strategy in the form of a **Writing skills** box, followed by a short practice activity. Strategies begin with things such as using subject pronouns with verbs, simple word order, and the use of capital letters for names.

Speaking

Speaking lessons provide a fun setting in which to review some of the language seen in the unit. A simple model dialog is presented by means of a short comic strip, with a different set of amusing characters appearing throughout each level of **Engage**.

After reading and listening to the dialog for the first time, students' attention is drawn to a particular area of pronunciation which is highlighted in a **Pronunciation** box. Specific examples from the dialog are given for students to listen and repeat. As a follow-up activity, there is an exercise featuring other examples taken from previous lessons or units of the book. To consolidate pronunciation work, students are then encouraged to practice the model dialog on the page.

> In pronunciation exercises, the emphasis is mostly on recognition, particularly in the early levels of **Engage**. However, it may be appropriate with some groups to ask the class to repeat the example sentences for extra practice before returning to the dialog. Teenage students often feel intimidated by pronunciation activities, so it can be a good idea to repeat as a whole class, rather than asking individual students to repeat individually.
>
> When practicing the model dialog, students will benefit from listening to the recording again. One way to organize this is to stop the CD after each sentence initially and have the whole class repeat in chorus. Do this as many times as necessary for your students to feel comfortable with the dialog.

Finally, students adapt the model dialog to make their own personalized versions, by substituting their own ideas for the words in blue. An initial written stage gives them the chance to prepare before performing the dialog in class—either in front of the whole group or, if appropriate, in pairs or small groups.

Review

Engage features a **Review** page after every Student Book unit in Levels 2 and 3. (In Starter and Level 1 this section appears after every two units.) Each vocabulary set and each grammar point is individually reviewed. A **Study skills** section introduces students to basic strategies for organizing and taking control of their own learning.

Engage Magazine

At the back of the **Student Book** is a **Magazine** section, which features puzzles, reading texts (**Reading for fun**) and guided projects.

The puzzles are designed as a fun extra activity to be completed when students reach the end of a **Grammar** page. In mixed-ability classes, they can be used as a reward for fast finishers. Alternatively, they can be used with the whole class as a warm-up or end-of-lesson activity. Each puzzle is linked to the vocabulary and grammar of the relevant **Grammar** page.

Reading for fun texts are meant to be exactly that—reading for the pleasure of reading. For this reason, they are included as optional extras, and there are no questions or exercises associated with them. Students should feel free to dip into these at any time during the year. However, the language used in each text means that they are best read after every three teaching units.

There are four **Project** pages in the **Magazine** section, each designed to review—and encourage active use of—the language taught in the previous three units. They are easily adapted to suit the needs of your students. They can be completed individually or in small groups, in class or as homework.

A clear model is shown on the page, broken down into short pieces of text. Students first read the model and match each piece of text with a category or question. This helps them identify the subject of each paragraph, and the language used. Step-by-step instructions are given on the page to guide students to produce their own projects.

Project work gives stronger students the opportunity for freer writing. This is always to be encouraged, even if it results in many more mistakes being made.

The weakest students, on the other hand, will sometimes need extra guidance to follow the model and adapt it. As with **Writing** lessons (see above), a useful first step is to look through the model with the students and help them identify the words and information that can be changed.

Other components

Workbook

For every *Student Book* unit, there are four pages of extra vocabulary and grammar practice in the *Workbook*.

Vocabulary pages all include an optional **Extend your vocabulary** exercise. The aim is to introduce students to some new words related to the main lexical set from the *Student Book*. For the sake of variety, the new words are used passively in the subsequent grammar practice activities, but they are not essential.

A five-page section at the end of the *Workbook* features four extracts from *Oxford Bookworms Library* readers, along with accompanying activities written especially for **Engage**. Extracts have been chosen carefully so that they allow for a gradual transition between levels. For example, the Starter *Workbook* has extracts from *Oxford Bookworms Starters*; Level 1 *Workbook* has two extracts from *Oxford Bookworms Starters*, and two from *Oxford Bookworms Library Stage 1*.

The vocabulary and grammar syllabus of **Engage** is broadly in line with the *Oxford Bookworms Library* syllabus. As a result, students nearing the end of **Engage Starter** will be able to enjoy readers from the **Starters** range. As they work their way through **Engage Level 1**, they will be able to make the transition to **Stage 1** readers, moving on to **Stage 2** for **Engage Level 2**, and **Stage 3** for **Engage Level 3**.

Teacher's Book

One of our principal aims in producing the material in **Engage** is clarity. We feel that the activities in the *Sudent Book* speak for themselves, and therefore require little explanation. As a result, the teaching notes are presented as step-by-step lesson plans. The notes for each activity simply state the aim, list the steps needed to complete the activity, and provide the

answers and, where appropriate, the audio script. There are no paragraphs or long explanations on the page.

For ease of reference, each page of teaching notes represents a page of the *Student Book*. The overall contents and aims of the unit are given in the **Unit summary** at the start of the notes for each unit; individual lesson aims are listed at the top of each page.

Within the notes there are occasional suggestions and background notes providing extra support for the teacher. These include ideas for warm-up activities at the start of a class; suggestions for simple follow-up or extension activities, graded according to level; background notes on matters of cultural or historical interest arising from reading or listening texts; and notes highlighting particular pitfalls to be aware of when teaching a given area of grammar.

Material from other components of **Engage** is cross-referenced at the relevant point within the notes, to enable you to see at a glance what other resources are available to you. In addition, a comprehensive *Workbook answer key* is provided at the back of the Teacher's Book.

Audio CDs

There are two *Audio CDs* accompanying each level of **Engage**. The recorded material includes all the vocabulary activities and presentation texts, all skills reading texts, listening activities, speaking dialogs and pronunciation exercises.

Mixed-Ability Worksheets

One photocopiable worksheet is provided as extension for each **Grammar** page of the *Student Book*. *Worksheets* all have three activities, graded as follows.

The first activity on each worksheet is designed to give extra support to weaker students who might be having difficulty in keeping up with the rest of the class. This activity is always at a slightly easier level than that of the corresponding *Student Book* page, and requires students to simply recognize correct forms and usage. The aim is to give more exposure to the target language and increase awareness of how it works, before demanding production.

The second activity is pitched at approximately the same level as the relevant page of the *Student Book*, and provides extra practice similar to that found in the *Workbook*.

The final activity on each worksheet gives stronger students the chance to try a less guided activity than those found in the *Student Book*. This will often mean producing whole sentences with a minimum of prompting, encouraging students to provide their own ideas.

Tests

The photocopiable **Tests** booklet provides one two-page test for each teaching unit. Tests are divided into three sections: **Vocabulary**, **Grammar** and **Reading**.

At the start of every test, both vocabulary sets from the corresponding **Student Book** unit are individually tested. The advantage of this is that it gives all students the opportunity to show what they have learned. Some students find it hard to remember grammar structures, but are able to remember individual words and phrases. By testing vocabulary at the level of individual words, we play to the strengths of these students and give them the motivation to learn more.

In the second section of the test, both grammar points from the teaching unit are tested using a variety of activity types. Questions range from simple recognition of form, through guided phrase and sentence-level production, so that all levels and abilities of students are catered for. Once again, the emphasis is firmly placed on encouraging students to show what they **know**, rather than what they **don't know**.

A reading comprehension accounts for the final activity in each test. A short reading passage places the relevant vocabulary and grammar in context, and a series of questions briefly test basic comprehension. Some students may perform well on this question despite a relatively poor performance on vocabulary and grammar questions.

The total number of points per test is 50. By looking at each section of the test in turn, you will be able to gain useful insights into the strengths and weaknesses of individual students.

Audio CDs

CD 1

Track	Contents
1	Title
2	Remember, page 4, Numbers, Exercise 2
3	Unit 1, page 9, Vocabulary, Exercise 1
4	Unit 1, page 10, Reading, Exercise 2
5	Unit 1, page 12, Vocabulary, Exercise 1
6	Unit 1, page 12, Vocabulary, Exercise 2
7	Unit 1, page 14, Reading
8	Unit 1, page 15, Listening, Exercise 1
9	Unit 2, page 17, Vocabulary, Exercise 1
10	Unit 2, page 18, Reading
11	Unit 2, page 20, Vocabulary, Exercise 1
12	Unit 2, page 22, Reading
13	Unit 2, page 23, Speaking, Exercise 1
14	Unit 2, page 23, Speaking, Exercise 2
15	Unit 2, page 23, Speaking, Exercise 3
16	Unit 3, page 25, Vocabulary, Exercise 1
17	Unit 3, page 26, Reading
18	Unit 3, page 28, Vocabulary, Exercise 1
19	Unit 3, page 28, Vocabulary, Exercise 2
20	Unit 3, page 30, Reading
21	Unit 3, page 31, Listening, Exercise 1
22	Unit 4, page 33, Vocabulary, Exercise 1
23	Unit 4, page 34, Reading
24	Unit 4, page 36, Vocabulary, Exercise 1
25	Unit 4, page 36, Vocabulary, Exercise 2
26	Unit 4, page 38, Reading
27	Unit 4, page 39, Listening, Exercise 2
28	Unit 4, page 39, Speaking, Exercise 1
29	Unit 4, page 39, Speaking, Exercise 2
30	Unit 4, page 39, Speaking, Exercise 3
31	Unit 5, page 41, Vocabulary, Exercise 1
32	Unit 5, page 42, Reading
33	Unit 5, page 44, Vocabulary, Exercise 1
34	Unit 5, page 44, Vocabulary, Exercise 2
35	Unit 5, page 46, Reading
36	Unit 5, page 47, Speaking, Exercise 1
37	Unit 5, page 47, Speaking, Exercise 2
38	Unit 5, page 47, Speaking, Exercise 3
39	Unit 6, page 49, Vocabulary, Exercise 1
40	Unit 6, page 50, Reading
41	Unit 6, page 52, Vocabulary, Exercise 1
42	Unit 6, page 52, Vocabulary, Exercise 2
43	Unit 6, page 54, Reading
44	Unit 6, page 55, Listening, Exercises 1, 2

CD 2

Track	Contents
1	Title
2	Unit 7, page 57, Vocabulary, Exercise 1
3	Unit 7, page 58, Reading
4	Unit 7, page 60, Vocabulary, Exercise 1
5	Unit 7, page 60, Vocabulary, Exercise 2
6	Unit 7, page 62, Reading
7	Unit 7, page 63, Listening, Exercises 1, 2
8	Unit 7, page 63, Speaking, Exercise 1
9	Unit 7, page 63, Speaking, Exercise 2
10	Unit 7, page 63, Speaking, Exercise 3
11	Unit 8, page 65, Vocabulary, Exercise 1
12	Unit 8, page 66, Reading
13	Unit 8, page 68, Vocabulary, Exercise 1
14	Unit 8, page 68, Vocabulary, Exercise 2
15	Unit 8, page 70, Reading
16	Unit 8, page 71, Listening, Exercise 1
17	Unit 9, page 73, Vocabulary, Exercise 1
18	Unit 9, page 74, Reading
19	Unit 9, page 76, Vocabulary, Exercise 1
20	Unit 9, page 76, Vocabulary, Exercise 2
21	Unit 9, page 78, Reading
22	Unit 9, page 79, Listening, Exercise 1
23	Unit 9, page 79, Speaking, Exercise 1
24	Unit 9, page 79, Speaking, Exercise 2
25	Unit 9, page 79, Speaking, Exercise 3
26	Unit 10, page 81, Vocabulary, Exercise 1
27	Unit 10, page 82, Reading
28	Unit 10, page 84, Vocabulary, Exercise 1
29	Unit 10, page 84, Vocabulary, Exercise 2
30	Unit 10, page 86, Reading
31	Unit 10, page 87, Speaking, Exercise 1
32	Unit 10, page 87, Speaking, Exercise 2
33	Unit 10, page 87, Speaking, Exercise 3
34	Unit 11, page 89, Vocabulary, Exercise 1
35	Unit 11, page 90, Reading
36	Unit 11, page 92, Vocabulary, Exercise 1
37	Unit 11, page 94, Reading
38	Unit 11, page 95, Listening, Exercise 2
39	Unit 11, page 95, Listening, Exercises 3, 4
40	Unit 11, page 95, Speaking, Exercise 1
41	Unit 11, page 95, Speaking, Exercise 2
42	Unit 11, page 95, Speaking, Exercise 3
43	Unit 12, page 97, Vocabulary, Exercise 1
44	Unit 12, page 98, Reading
45	Unit 12, page 100, Vocabulary, Exercise 1
46	Unit 12, page 100, Vocabulary, Exercise 2

Remember

Unit summary

Active vocabulary
- numbers 100–1000
- dates
- feelings: angry, happy, nervous, scared, surprised, tired
- food: apples, cheese, chicken, milk, muffins, soda, yogurts
- clothes: boots, cap, gloves, hat, jacket, jersey, shirt, shorts, sneakers, sunglasses, T-shirt
- parts of the body: body, eyes, feet, hands, head
- adjectives: cheap, expensive, hard, heavy, light, long, new, old, short, small, soft, thick
- appearance: blond/curly/wavy hair, brown eyes, short, tall

Skills
- Listening to numbers 1–1000
- Describing classmates and objects

Grammar
- *some* and *any*
- object pronouns
- Present progressive (affirmative, negative and questions)
- Present simple (affirmative, negative and questions)

Numbers 100–1000

> ### Aims
> Review numbers 100–1000

1 Practice numbers 100–1000
- Write the numbers in words.

Answers
1 one hundred twelve
2 seven hundred thirty-four
3 two hundred thirty-nine
4 six hundred fifty
5 three hundred thirty-two
6 six hundred seventy-seven
7 five hundred ninety-one
8 a thousand

2 Practice recognition of numbers 0–1000
- Listen and circle the numbers you hear.

Answers / Audio CD 1 track 2

1	160	4	223
2	413	5	190
3	866		

Dates

> ### Aims
> Review months and ordinal numbers
> Personalization of dates

1 Practice of months and ordinal numbers
- Write the dates.

Answers
1 June twenty-first
2 August eleventh
3 September second
4 April thirtieth
5 December seventh

2 Personalization; practice of months and ordinal numbers
- Write the date of your birthday.

Feelings

> ### Aims
> Review and practice feelings
> Review simple present *be*, simple present, simple past *be*

1 Practice feelings
- Read the sentences.
- Fill in the blanks with the adjectives in the box.

Answers

1	happy	4	angry
2	surprised	5	tired
3	nervous	6	scared

Food

Aims
Review and practice food vocabulary
Review *there is / there are* (affirmative and negative)
Review and practice *some / any*

1 Practice food vocabulary

- Look at the pictures.
- Label the pictures with the words in the box.

Answers
1	cheese	5	apples
2	chicken	6	muffins
3	milk	7	yogurts
4	soda		

2 Review *there is / there are*; practice *some / any*

- Read the sentences.
- Fill in the blanks with *some* or *any*.

Answers
1	some	4	any
2	any	5	some
3	some	6	any

Object pronouns

Aims
Review and practice personal and object pronouns

1 Grammar chart: personal and object pronouns

- Fill in the chart with the missing pronouns.

Answers
1	me	5	it
2	you	6	us
3	he	7	you
4	her	8	them

2 Controlled practice personal and object pronouns

- Look at the pictures and read the sentences.
- Fill in the blanks with the words in the box.

Answers
1	her	4	us
2	me	5	him
3	them		

Clothes

Aims
Review and practice clothes vocabulary

1 Practice of clothes vocabulary

- Read the letter and look at the pictures.
- Fill in the blanks with items of clothing that Matt needs.

Answers
1	sneakers	6	boots
2	sunglasses	7	jersey
3	cap	8	jacket
4	shorts	9	hat
5	T-shirt	10	gloves

Parts of the body

Aims
Review parts of the body
Review and practice clothes vocabulary

1 Review parts of the body; practice clothes vocabulary

- Read the parts of the body.
- Fill in the blanks with the clothes from the exercise above.

Answers
1	cap	6	jersey
2	hat	7	jacket
3	sunglasses	8	gloves
4	shorts	9	sneakers
5	T-shirt	10	boots

Adjectives (objects)

Aims
Review and practice adjectives to describe objects
Review present progressive
Review *there is / there are*,
Review simple present *be*

1 Practice of adjectives to describe objects

- Look at the picture and read the text.
- Fill in the blanks with the adjectives in box.

Answers

1	old	4	thick
2	expensive	5	soft
3	long	6	heavy

2 Practice of adjectives and their opposites

- Read the adjectives and write the opposites.

Answers

1	new	4	short
2	hard	5	cheap
3	light		

Invitations

> **Aims**
> Review and practice the language of invitations

1 Practice the language of invitations

- Read the dialog.
- Fill in the blanks with the phrases in the box.

Answers

1	Would you like to	3	Let's
2	Sure	4	I'm sorry

Appearance

> **Aims**
> Review of appearance vocabulary
> Review *have*, present progressive

1 Review of appearance vocabulary

- Look at the picture and read the sentences.
- Write the names of the person next to each sentence.

Answers

1	Anita	5	Matt
2	Anita	6	Lucio
3	Katie	7	Anita and Katie
4	Lucio and Matt	8	Anita

Extra activity (all classes)

Students personalize practice of appearance vocabulary

- Ask students to write three sentences that describe someone in the class, e.g. *He has curly hair*.
- Students read out their first sentence to the class. Can the class guess who the person is?
- If they can't the student reads out their next sentence and so on until the class guesses.

Present progressive

> **Aims**
> Review and practice present progressive (affirmative and negative)

1 Grammar chart: present progressive (affirmative and negative)

> **Note:**
> - We make the present progressive with *be* (+ *not*) + the *–ing* form of the verb.
> - The present progressive describes actions happening right now, e.g. *I'm listening to music right now*.
> - See Grammar summary page 113.

- Read the chart and fill in the blanks.

Answers

1	am	2	is	3	isn't	4	are	5	aren't

2 Controlled practice of present progressive (affirmative and negative)

- Look at the picture on page 6.
- Read the sentence skeletons.
- Write sentences in the present progressive.

Answers

1 Katie is dancing.
  She isn't singing.
2 Lucio isn't eating a burger.
  He is eating French fries.
3 Matt is laughing.
  He isn't shouting.
4 Anita isn't drinking milk.
  She is drinking soda.

3 Grammar chart: present progressive (yes / no questions, wh- questions and short answers)

Note:
- We make *yes / no* questions with the present progressive by inverting *be* and the pronoun.
- We make short answers with *Yes / No* + subject pronoun + *be*. We make *wh-* questions with the present progressive by adding a *wh-* word to the beginning of a *yes / no* question, e.g. *What are you listening to?*
- See Grammar summary page 113.

- Read the chart and fill in the blanks.

Answers
1	Are	5	isn't
2	are	6	are
3	aren't	7	is
4	Is		

4 Controlled practice of present progressive (yes / no questions, wh- questions and short answers)

- Read the skeleton question.
- Write questions in the present progressive.
- Look at the picture on page 6 and answer the questions.

Answers
1 Is Katie wearing a red shirt? Yes, she is.
2 Is Anita dancing? No, she isn't.
3 Are Lucio and Matt wearing blue sneakers? No, they aren't.
4 What is Anita drinking? She's drinking a soda.
5 Is Lucio eating a burger? No, he isn't.

Simple present

Aims
Review and practice simple present (affirmative and negative)

1 Grammar chart: simple present (affirmative and negative)

Note:
- The form of the simple present is the same for *I, you* (singular) / *we / you* (plural) / *they*.
- We add *-s* or *-es* to the verb for the *he / she / it* forms.

- When a verb ends in *-o, -s, -sh, -ss, -z, -x* or *-ch*, we add *-es* to the verb, e.g. *watch* ➡ *watches*.
- When a verb ends in *-y*, we replace the *y* with *i* and add *-es*, e.g. *carry* ➡ *carries*.
- Some verbs are irregular and have their own *he / she / it* forms, e.g. *is* (be), *has* (have).
- We make the negative form of the simple present with *don't / doesn't* + the infinitive of the verb, e.g. *He doesn't know.*
- We use the simple present to talk about habits or things we do regularly.
- See Grammar summary page 113.

- Fill in the blanks in the chart.

Answers
1	don't	2	doesn't

2 Controlled practice of simple present (affirmative)

- Read the e-mail and fill in the blanks with the simple present form of the verbs in parentheses.

Answers
1	lives	4	drives
2	get up	5	go
3	have		

3 Controlled practice of simple present (negative)

- Read the sentences and make them negative.

Answers
1 Katie doesn't live 6km from the city.
2 They don't go to the movies.
3 They don't have breakfast with Katie's brother.
4 Katie's dad doesn't drive them to the beach.
5 Matt doesn't get up late.

4 Grammar chart: simple present (*yes / no* questions, *wh-* questions and short answers)

> **Note:**
> * We make *yes / no* questions in the simple present with *do / does* + subject + verb (base form), e.g. *Do you play tennis?* NOT ~~You play tennis?~~
> * The auxiliary verb *do / does* must agree with the subject in questions, e.g. *Does he like this?* and *Do they like this?*
>   The main verb is always in its base form e.g. *Does he get up early?* NOT ~~Does he gets up early?~~
> * In short answers, we use the auxiliary verb *do / does*, *don't / doesn't* and not the main verb in the question, e.g. *Do you go to school? Yes, I do.* NOT ~~Yes, I go.~~
> * We make *wh-* questions in the simple present by adding a *wh-* word (*How, What, When, Where, Why*) to the beginning of a *yes / no* question.

* Fill in the blanks in the chart.

Answers

1	Do	4	does
2	don't	5	does
3	Does		

Extra activity (stronger classes)

Students practice *yes / no* questions in a game.

* Students work in small groups.
* Ask students to think of a job.
* Students mime the actions of their job to each other.
* Students take turns to ask each other *yes / no* questions to try and guess the job, e.g. *Do you work outside? Do you work with children?*

5 Controlled practice of simple present (*wh-* questions)

* Read the dialog.
* Read the skeleton questions in parenthesis.
* Write the questions in the simple present.

Answers

1 Where do you live, Katie?
2 Where does Matt live?
3 What do you do on the weekend?
4 What kind of music do you like?

Review it!

1 Play a game; review grammar and vocabulary in the Remember unit

* Work in pairs.
* Throw the dice and answer the questions.

➡ **Workbook page 2**

1 Our world

Unit summary

Active vocabulary

- sports and hobbies: acting, painting, playing in a band, playing soccer, running, scuba diving, shopping, working on a computer
- adjectives: awful, boring, cool, exciting, fun, hard, interesting, OK
- town vocabulary: entertainment, houses, litter, noise, open spaces, pollution, tall buildings, traffic
- transport: bicycle, car, truck
- other: beach, club, cyber café, dislikes

Passive vocabulary

- nouns: air, apartment, balcony, cafés, fast food restaurant, floor, green space, group, guitar, life / lives, live music, mall, marathon, movie theater, music club, neighbourhood, painting, park, playing basketball, open space, playing tennis, riding a bicycle, scuba diving, skateboarding, skater, skating rink, soccer, sports field, stadium, traffic, trash, village, water sports
- adjectives: clean, dirty, cool
- verbs: laugh
- other: best of both worlds

Grammar

- gerunds (-ing form)
- much / many / a lot of

Skills

- Reading about people looking for friends
- Reading young people's comments about where they live
- Reading about someone who lives in a village and in a city
- Listen to a conversation about a town
- Writing a postcard about a place

Cross-curricular

- sport; geography

Values

- multicultural societies; environmental awareness

Introducing the topic

Vocabulary

Aims

Present and practice vocabulary of sports and hobbies
Recycle adjectives describing likes and dislikes
Model gerunds (–ing forms)

Warm-up

Books closed. Which are the most popular sports and hobbies in the class? Who has got the most unusual hobby?

1 Presentation of vocabulary set: sports and hobbies

- Look at the photos.
- Write the correct number next to sport and hobby.
- Listen, check and repeat.

Answers / Audio CD 1 Track 3

1 playing soccer
2 running
3 scuba diving
4 working on a computer
5 painting
6 playing in a band
7 shopping
8 acting

Recycling

2 Practice and review *be*; exposure to gerunds (–ing forms)

- Read the adjectives.
- Write sentences about the sports and hobbies with the adjectives.

Answers
Students' own answers

Extend your vocabulary (Workbook page 4)

➡ **Workbook page 4**

Exploring the topic

> **Aims**
>
> Present and practice *like / enjoy / love / don't like / hate + -ing* form
> Read a text about teenagers' likes and dislikes
> Review sports and hobbies

Reading

 **Audio CD 1 Track 4**

Warm-up

Books closed. Do students have any online friends? Where did they meet them? Which countries are they from? What do they talk about together? In which country would students like to make a friend?

1 **Comprehension (first reading); exposure to *like / enjoy / love / don't like / hate + -ing* form**

- Read the words.
- Read the text quickly, looking for the information that appears in the text.
- Check (✓) the information that appears in the text.

Answers

name, age, likes, dislikes

2 **Comprehension (second reading)**

- Read the statements.
- Read and listen to the text.
- Fill in the blanks with the names of the teenagers.

Answers

1	Anh	5	Carlos
2	Carlos	6	Liliana
3	Anh	7	Carlos
4	Andreas	8	Anh, Liliana

Extra activity (stronger classes)

Practice of *like / enjoy / love / don't like / hate + -ing* form

- Ask students to look at their answers in exercise 2.
- Read the sentences from exercise 2 and ask students to justify their answers using words from the text, e.g.
  T: Anh doesn't like running.
  S: It says, "She hates running!"

Answers

1 She hates running.
2 He loves playing soccer.
3 She loves painting.
4 He thinks acting is fun.
5 He thinks working on a computer is cool.
6 She hates shopping. She thinks it's boring.
7 His singing is terrible. His friends laugh at him.
8 Anh thinks scuba diving is fun. Liliana thinks scuba diving is exciting.

Grammar

1 Grammar chart: gerunds (*-ing* form)

Note:
- If we use another verb after *like / enjoy / love / don't like / hate*, we use the *-ing* form of the verb, e.g. *I love singing*. NOT ~~I love sing.~~
  See Grammar summary page 113.

2 Controlled practice of *like / enjoy / love / don't like / hate*

- Read the sentences.
- Write the correct icon next to each sentence.

Answers

1	☹	4	☺
2	☺	5	☺
3	☹	6	☹

Take note!

Spelling rules for *-ing* forms

We make the *-ing* form:
- of regular verbs by adding *-ing*, e.g. *play* ➡ *playing*
- of verbs ending in one vowel + one consonant by doubling the final consonant and adding *-ing*, e.g. *shop* ➡ *shopping*. Common exceptions to this rule are words ending in *-l*, e.g. *travel* ➡ *traveling*
- of verbs ending in *-e* by removing the *-e* and adding *-ing*, e.g. *write* ➡ *writing*

3 Controlled practice of gerunds (*-ing* form)

- Read the sentences.
- Fill in the blanks with the *-ing* form of the correct verbs in the box.

Answers

1	riding	4	reading
2	playing	5	running
3	shopping	6	doing

4 Grammar chart: *-ing* form + *be* + adjective

Note:
- We can make *-ing* forms the subject of a sentence.
- The verb is always singular, e.g. *Shopping is boring*. NOT ~~Shopping are boring.~~
- See Grammar summary page 113.

5 Controlled practice of *-ing* form + *be* + adjective

- Look at the picture and read the skeleton sentences.
- Write sentences using the *-ing* form of the verbs.

Answers

1 Playing tennis is hard.
2 Painting is fun.
3 Skateboarding is exciting.
4 Playing in a band is cool.
5 Watching TV is boring.
6 Reading is interesting.

Finished?

Fast finishers can do Puzzle 1A on page 105

Answer

He likes playing computer games.

Over to you!

6 Personalization; written and oral practice of *love*, *like* and *hate* + gerund (*-ing form*)

- Write two true sentences and one false sentence using the verbs *love*, *like* and *hate* + *-ing* form.
- Take turns to tell the class (see example).
- Are the students' statements true or false?

➡ **Workbook page 5**

➡ **Mixed Ability Worksheets page 2**

Building the topic

Vocabulary

> ### Aims
> Present and practice town vocabulary
> Model *much / many / a lot of*
> Present countable and uncountable nouns

Warm-up

Books closed. Do students like where they live? Why? Why not? Would they prefer to live in a city or a village? What are the good / bad things about living in each place?

1 Presentation of vocabulary set: town vocabulary

- Look at the two photos.
- Write the correct number next to each word or phrase.
- Listen, check and repeat.

🎧 **Answers / Audio CD 1 track 5**

1 tall buildings	5 traffic
2 pollution	6 litter
3 noise	7 houses
4 entertainment	8 open spaces

2 Vocabulary practice; exposure to *much / many / a lot of*

- Read and listen to the comments.
- Write the number of the correct picture next to the comments.

🎧 **Answers / Audio CD 1 track 6**

1 Like most big cities, there's a lot of pollution. But I love it here. It's really exciting.
There are a lot of cars, trucks and buses, so there's a lot of noise.
There are a lot of tall building and they are building more every day.
There's a lot of entertainment. There are movie theatres, music clubs and cafés. It's great.

2 There isn't much traffic in my village. There are only about fifty cars!
There are a lot of open spaces where I live. It's really nice.
There are a lot of small houses, but we don't have tall buildings.
There isn't much litter in the streets. It's very clean.

3 Practice countable and uncountable nouns

- Read the words.
- Write C (countable) or U (uncountable) next to each word.

Answers

1	U	5	C
2	U	6	U
3	C	7	U
4	U	8	C

Extra activity (all classes)

Practice of countable and uncountable nouns

- Write the list of words on the board.

1	pop	16	key
2	car	17	water
3	paint	18	sugar
4	dog	19	balloon
5	milk	20	money
6	time	21	banana
7	music	22	bicycle
8	salt	23	tea
9	student	24	tree
10	cheese	25	paper
11	bridge	26	soap
12	coffee	27	hair
13	rice	28	CD
14	lemonade	29	sound
15	oranges		

- In pairs, students decide if they are C (countable) or U (uncountable).
- Give students a minute to do as many as possible.

Answers

1	U	16	C
2	C	17	U
3	U	18	U
4	C	19	C
5	U	20	U
6	U	21	C
7	U	22	C
8	U	23	U
9	C	24	C
10	U	25	U
11	C	26	U
12	U	27	U
13	U	28	C
14	U	29	U
15	C		

Extend your vocabulary (Workbook page 6)

➜ **Workbook page 6**

Grammar

Aims

Present and practice *much / many / a lot of* to talk about quantity

Review *there is / there are* (affirmative and negative)

Review *be* (questions)

Talk about quantity

1 Grammar chart: *much / many / a lot of*

Note:
- We use *how much* and *how many* to ask about quantity.
- We use *how many ... ?* with countable nouns and *how much ... ?* with uncountable nouns.
- We use *there are + a lot of +* the plural form of countable nouns.
- We use *there's + a lot of +* uncountable nouns.
- We use *there aren't + many +* the plural form of countable nouns.
- We use *there isn't + much +* uncountable nouns.
- See Grammar summary page 113.

2 Controlled practice of *much / many / a lot of*

- Read the sentences.
- Circle the correct word or phrase.

Answers

1	a lot of	4	many
2	many	5	a lot of
3	a lot of	6	many

3 Review of *there is / there are* (affirmative and negative); controlled practice of *much / many / a lot of*

- Look at the picture and read the sentences.
- Fill in the blanks with *much*, *many* or *a lot of*.

Answers

1	a lot of	4	many
2	many	5	a lot of
3	a lot of	6	much

Finished?

Fast finishers can do Puzzle 1B on page 105

Answers

There are 26 people on the bus.

You are the bus driver so his / her name is your name.

4 Review questions; controlled practice of *how much ... ? / how many ... ?*

- Read the answers.
- Write questions using *How much / How many*.

Answers

1 How many CDs do you have?
2 How much homework do you do?
3 How many friends have you got?
4 How many parks are there in your neighbourhood?
5 How much noise is there in your house.
6 How many (hours of TV do you watch?)

Over to you!

5 Personalization; practice of *how much ... ? / how many ... ?*

- Look at the questions in exercise 4 again.
- Take turns to ask your partner the questions and respond appropriately (see example).

➡ **Workbook page 7**

➡ **Mixed Ability Worksheets page 3**

Living English

Aims
Read about a teenager who lives in the city and the country.
Identify key words in a reading text.
Listen and identify facts in two teenagers' conversation.
Write a postcard about where you are living.

Reading

 Audio CD 1 track 7

Cultural note

- **Greece** is a country in south-east Europe. Its population is 10.6 million and its capital is Athens. The official language is Greek.

Warm-up

- Books closed. Do students have relatives who live in a different type of place (e.g. a village or a city) than them? Do they visit them? What do they like / dislike about the place where their relatives live?

Before you read

1 Pre-reading task

- Look at the picture and the title of the text.
- Answer the question.

Answers
Nikos lives in a village AND in a city.

While you read

2 Comprehension task (first reading)

- Read the questions.
- Read the article.
- Write the answers.

Answers
The city: He likes going out with other young people. He likes the sports stadiums because he loves watching sport.

The village: There are a lot of open spaces and he likes going to the beach near his village.

After you read

3 Presentation and practice of reading skill (second reading)

- Read the reading skills box.

> **Reading skills: Key words**
> Looking for key words in a text can help you to read it more quickly and understand the main ideas in each paragraph.

- Read the main ideas in the article.
- Read the article quickly and look for key words for the ideas.
- Write the key words next to each idea.

Answers
1 people, population, going out, young people, friends
2 tall building, apartment, rooms, balconies, house, one floor, other houses
3 going out, movie theatres, cafés, dance clubs, cyber cafés, stadiums, sports fields, restaurants, open spaces, beach

4 Detailed comprehension task (third reading)

- Read the sentences.
- Read the article again.
- Fill in the blanks with a word or words from the text.

Answers
1 the summer   5 watching
2 big   6 cyber cafés
3 200   7 beach
4 friends

Listening

1 Comprehension task (first listening)

- Listen to the dialog and answer the question.

🎧 **Audio CD 1 Track 8**

Deb:	Hi. Welcome to the school. My name's Deb.
Mike:	My name's Mike.
Deb:	So, where are you from, Mike?
Mike:	I'm from New York.
Deb:	Wow! It's really different here, I guess.
Mike:	Well, it's really quiet. And there isn't much entertainment.
Deb:	I know. What do you like to do?
Mike:	I love playing tennis. That's my favorite thing.
Deb:	Really? It's mine too! There's a really good tennis club in the next town. I go there three days a week.
Mike:	Great! I like acting too.
Deb:	There's a good theater group at the school. My friend Tina goes.
Mike:	Cool! Do you do much homework at this school?
Deb:	No, we don't do much. Just a couple of hours a day.
Mike:	That's not too bad. I think I like being here!

Answer

Playing tennis

2 Detailed comprehension of listening text (second listening)

- Read the sentences.
- Fill in the blanks with the words in the box.

Answers

1 New York
2 quiet
3 entertainment
4 club
5 acting
6 theater
7 homework

Writing

Cultural note

- **Tucson** is a city in Arizona in North America. Its population is about 0.9 million. It is the 32nd largest city in the United States.

1 General comprehension of writing model

- Read the postcard quickly.
- Answer the questions.

Answers

The postcard's from Tucson.
Yes, she is.

2 Detailed comprehension of writing model

- Read the postcard again.
- Underline Anna's likes in red and her dislikes in blue.
- Fill in the chart with what Ann likes and doesn't like.

Answers

Name of place	Tucson
She likes:	nice houses, green spaces, not much pollution or litter, lots of places to play soccer, going to the stadium and watching soccer games, school: the kids are great and the teachers are nice
She doesn't like:	not many cafés or places to meet, not any beaches

3 Preparation for personalized writing

- Imagine you are living in a different place.
- Copy the chart and fill it in with information about the place and the things you like and don't like about it.

4 Personalized writing

- Use the writing model and your notes in exercise 3.
- Write a postcard from the place you are living.

➡ **Tests page 2**

1 **Review**

Vocabulary

1 1 playing soccer
2 acting
3 playing in a band.
4 working on a computer
5 shopping
6 painting
7 Scuba diving
8 running

2 1 tall buildings
2 pollution
3 entertainment
4 litter
5 traffic
6 open spaces
7 noise
8 houses

Grammar

1 1 He enjoys spending time with his parents.
2 He loves acting.
3 He likes watching movies.
4 He doesn't like doing homework.
5 He enjoys helping other people.
6 He loves listening to music.

2 1 How much noise is there?
   There isn't much noise.
2 How many people are there?
   There are a lot of people.
3 How much pollution is there?
   There isn't much pollution.
   How many parks are there?
   There are a lot of parks.
   How many buildings are there?
   There are a lot of buildings.
   How much entertainment is there?
   There isn't much entertainment.

Study skills

1 1 Pages 2 and 3
2 Page 119
3 Page 105
4 Page 113

2 All about me

Unit summary

Active vocabulary

- activities: eat fast food, go climbing, go to school, listen to music, play an instrument, play basketball, read magazines, watch movies
- daily activities: get dressed, get home, get up, go to bed, go to school, have dinner
- household chores: clean (your) room, cut the grass, make (your) bed, make lunch, put away (your things), set the table, take out the garbage, wash the dishes
- places in a house: bedroom, kitchen, dining room, yard
- nouns: blogname, bone, deodorant, disaster, dinosaur, laboratories, lake, poison, snake
- adjectives: deep
- verbs: chat, come home, dust, lock, look for, take out, turn off
- unusual jobs: dinosaur duster, golf ball diver, odor judge, page turner, snake venom extractor

Grammar

- Simple present and present progressive (affirmative, negative and questions)
- *have to*

Skills

- Reading a chat session between old friends
- Reading about unusual jobs
- Writing your online profile
- Talking about the type of music and books you like
- Using appropriate sentence stress

Cross-curricular

- geography, music

Values

- citizenship

Introducing the topic

Vocabulary

Aims

Present and practice activities vocabulary
Review everyday activities

Warm-up

Books closed. Ask students to imagine they could see through a keyhole into their rooms. What would you see if you looked right now? Give students a minute to write a list of as many things as possible.

1 Presentation of vocabulary set: activities

- Look at the pictures of the bedrooms through the keyholes.
- Write the correct number next to each activity.
- Listen, check and repeat.

🎧 Answers / Audio CD 1 track 9

1 go climbing	3 go to school
1 play basketball	3 listen to music
2 play an instrument	3 watch movies
2 eat fast food	3 read magazines

Recycling

2 Review of everyday activities

- Look at the verbs.
- Write the time that you do the activities every day.

Answers
Students' own answers

3 Personalization; extension of everyday activities vocabularly

- Add two more verbs to the wheel.
- Add the time you do the activities every day.

Possible answers
go to sleep / wake up

Extend your vocabulary (Workbook page 8)

➡ Workbook page 8

Exploring the topic

Aims
Present simple present (affirmative, negative and questions) and present progressive (affirmative, negative and questions)
Review activities vocabulary

Reading

 Audio CD 1 track 10

Cultural note

- **Iceland** is an island country in the northern Atlantic Ocean. Its population is about 300,000. Its capital is Reykjavik. Its location means that fish are an important part of Icelandic cooking.

Warm-up

Books closed. Do students have any old friends who have moved away from their area? Where did they move to? Why did they move? Are they still in contact with their old friends?

1 General comprehension (first reading); exposure to simple present and present progressive

- Read the statements.
- Read the text and circle T (True) or F (False).

Answers

1	T	5	T
2	T	6	F
3	T	7	F
4	F	8	T

2 Detailed comprehension (second reading)

- Read and listen to the text.
- Match the beginnings and ends of the sentences.

Answers

1	C	4	B
2	E	5	D
3	A		

Grammar

Aims

Present, contrast and practice simple present and present progressive (affirmative, negative and questions)
Talk about regular activities and things that are happening right now

1 **Grammar chart: simple present and present progressive (affirmative, negative and questions)**

Note:
- We use the simple present to talk about things that happen regularly.
- We use phrases such as *every evening*, *on the weekend*, with the simple present.
- We also use adverbs of frequency such as *never*, *sometimes*, *often*, *usually*, *always* with the simple present.
- We use the present progressive to talk about things that are happening right now.
- We can use *right now* with the present progressive to indicate we are talking about this moment.
- See Grammar summary page 113.

2 **Controlled practice of simple present and present progressive (affirmative)**

- Look at the pictures of what Yoshi Zang does Monday to Friday and what he is doing right now.
- Read the sentences.
- Circle the correct sentence.

Answers

1	a	4	b
2	a	5	b
3	b		

3 **Further practice of simple present and present progressive (affirmative)**

- Read the text about Yoshi and notice the phrases in each sentence, e.g. *usually* or *right now*.
- Fill in the blanks with the simple present or present progressive of the verb in parentheses.

Answers

1	work	5	makes
2	'm drawing	6	's wearing
3	helps	7	go
4	looks	8	meet

Finished?

Fast finishers can do Puzzle 2A on page 105.

Answers

go**es**	**p**lay
listens	drive
reads	sin**gs**
watch**es**	**g**et up

He's sleeping.

Over to you!

4 **Personalization; oral practice of simple present (affirmative and negative); review *like* + *-ing* form**

- Write three things you see through the keyhole into your room.
- Show them to your partner.
- Take turns to tell your partner about the things (see example) using *like* + *-ing* where possible.

Extra activity (stronger classes)

Practice simple present and present progressive (*yes / no* questions)

- This is an extension of an extra activity from the *Remember* unit. Students practice simple present and present progressive *yes / no* questions and play a guessing game.
- Ask students to think of a job.
- Students mime actions related to their job to each other.
- Students take turns to ask each other *yes / no* questions to try and guess the job, e.g. *Do you work in an office? In your mime, are you holding a pen?*

➡ **Workbook page 9**

➡ **Mixed Ability Worksheets page 4**

Building the topic
Vocabulary

Aims
Present and practice household chores
Model *have to* for obligation.

Warm-up

Books closed. What chores do students have to do at home? How often do they do them? Do they like doing them? What happens if they don't do them? Do they ever offer to help with household chores?

1 **Presentation of vocabulary set: household chores; exposure to *have to***

- Look at the pictures.
- Fill in the blanks with the phrases in the box.
- Listen, check and repeat.

Answers / Audio CD 1 Track 11

1   make (my) bed
2   wash the dishes
3   clean (my) room
4   put away
5   set the table
6   take out the garbage
7   make lunch
8   cut the grass

2 **Vocabulary practice**

- Read the chart.
- Write the correct chore next to each room.

Answers
bedroom – make your bed, clean your room, put away your things
kitchen – wash the dishes, take out the garbage, make lunch
dining room – set the table
yard – cut the grass

Extend your vocabulary (Workbook page 10)

➡ **Workbook page 10**

Grammar

Aims
Present and practice *have to* (affirmative, negative and questions)
Talk about obligation

1 Grammar chart: *have to*

Note:
- We use the affirmative of *have to* to talk about obligation.
- We use the negative of *have to* to say that you have a choice, e.g. *I don't have to make lunch,* means I can make lunch if I want to, but it is not obligatory.
- The form of *have to* is the same for *I, you* (singular) / *we* / *you* (plural) / *they.*
- We use *has to* with *he* / *she* / *it.*
- We make the negative of *have to* with *don't* / *doesn't* + *have to,* e.g. *I don't have to wear a school uniform.*
- We make questions with *Do* / *Does,* e.g. *Does he have to go?*
- See Grammar summary page 113.

2 Controlled practice of *have to* (affirmative)

- Read the sentences.
- Fill in the blanks with *have to* / *has to.*

Answers
1 has to
2 have to
3 have to
4 has to
5 have to

3 Controlled practice of *have to* (affirmative and negative)

- Look at the pictures.
- Fill in the blanks with correct affirmative (✓) or negative (✗) from of *have to.*

Answers

1	has to	4 don't have to
2	doesn't have to	5 doesn't have to
3	have to	6 has to

Extra activity (all classes)

Practice of *have to*

- Write the sentences on the board.
- Students fill in the gaps with *has to* / *doesn't have to.*
- Stronger classes can write their own sentences.
  1 A nurse ...... like helping people.
  2 A doctor ...... study biology.
  3 A lawyer ...... be a man.
  4 A pilot ...... like traveling.
  5 A flight attendant ...... be polite.
  6 A vet ...... like animals.
  7 A secretary ...... study medicine.

Answers

1	has to	5	has to
2	has to	6	has to
3	doesn't have to	7	doesn't have to
4	has to		

4 Further practice of *have to* (affirmative and negative)

- Read the college rules.
- Rewrite the imperative sentences with *have to* and *don't have to.*

Answers
1 You have to lock your room.
2 You have to turn off the lights after midnight.
3 You have to come home before 11 p.m.
4 You have to put away your things.
5 You don't have to cut the grass.
6 You don't have to clean your room.
7 You don't have to put out the garbage.

Finished?

Fast finishers can do Puzzle 2B on page 105.

Answers

a	make (your) bed	d	set the table
b	clean (your) room	e	wash the dishes
c	cut the grass	f	take out the garbage

Over to you!

5 Personalization; oral practice of *have to* (questions and short answers)

- Write three chores you have to do.
- Take turns to ask questions using *have to.*
- Respond appropriately (see example).

➡ Workbook page 11

➡ Mixed Ability Worksheets page 15

Living English

Aims

Read about unusual jobs
Practice organizing writing into paragraphs
Use a chart to plan your writing
Talk about things you like and what you are doing right now
Use appropriate sentence stress

Reading

 Audio CD 1 track 12

Cultural note

- Carnegie Hall is a concert hall in New York City. It was built in 1890 and is a famous place for classical and popular music.

Warm-up

Books closed. Do students know any adults with unusual jobs? What do they do? Would they like to do this job? Have they heard of any other unusual jobs?

Before you read

1 Pre-reading task

- Look at the photos and answer the question.

Answers

Students' own answers

While you read

2 General comprehension (first reading)

- Look at the photos.
- Read the article quickly.
- Match a photo to each text.

Answers

1	D	4	A
2	B	5	C
3	E		

After you read

3 Detailed comprehension (second reading)

- Read the questions.
- Read the article again.
- Write the answers.

Answers

1 He's a "golf ball diver".
2 He's collecting balls in a lake.
3 She's smelling a deodorant.
4 She's a "page turner".
5 She's cleaning an animal's bone.
6 A "dinosaur duster" has to clean dinosaur bones.
7 He's a "snake venom extractor".

Writing

1 Present of the writing skill

- Read the Writing skills box.

> **Writing skills: Paragraphs**
> A paragraph is a group of sentences which deal with one subject. All the sentences are connected to the subject. Paragraphs are one of the most important tools in writing. They help you organize ideas logically and indicate to the reader when there is a change of subject.

2 Identification of the main topic in each paragraph

- Read the profile.
- Match each paragraph to each main idea.

Answers

Usual activities 2
Personal information 1
Interests 3

3 Detailed comprehension of writing model

- Read the profile again.
- Fill in the chart with information about Marie.

Answers

Personal data

Name: Marie	Country: United States
Nickname: India	Town: New Jersey
Age: 18	

Usual activities

(morning) get up very early and go to school.
(afternoon) have to make my bed and put my things away.
(evening) meet my friends, or surf the Net.

Interests

reading fashion magazines and listening to hip hop.

Activities right now

listening to a new band called Klinical on my computer.

4 Preparation for personalized writing

- Copy the chart.
- Fill it in with information about you your usual activities, interests and what you are doing right now.

5 Personalized writing

- Write your profile.
- Use the writing model and the chart in exercise 4.

Speaking

1 First listening

- Look at the pictures and read the model dialog.
- Listen and read.

🎧 **Audio CD 1 track 13**

2 Presentation of pronunciation point

> **Pronunciation: Stress**
> We usually stress verbs, nouns and questions words in sentences. This means we pronounce them slightly more loudly and for longer than the other words in the sentence. Understanding sentence stress correctly will help your listening and speaking skills.

- Read the examples in the Pronunciation box.
- Listen to the examples and repeat, copying the stressed words in bold.

🎧 **Audio CD 1 track 14**

3 Pronunciation practice

- Read the sentences.
- Circle the stressed word(s) in each sentence.
- Listen, check and repeat.

🎧 **Answers / Audio CD 1 track 15**

1	Where, live	3	like, swimming
2	student	4	What, books, like

4 Dialog practice

- Practice the model dialog with another student.
- Change roles and practice again.

5 Dialog personalization and practice

- Look at the words in blue in the model dialog.
- Think of different kinds of music and books.
- Replace the blue words with your ideas to make a new dialog.
- Practice the dialog with another student.

➡ Tests page 4

2 Review

Vocabulary

1
1 eat
2 listen
3 read
4 go
5 play
6 go

2
1 put away (your things)
2 clean (you) room
3 set the table
4 wash the dishes
5 make (your) bed
6 take out the garbage
7 make lunch
8 cut the grass

Grammar

1
1 works
2 reads
3 practices
4 joins
5 are rehearsing
6 are wearing
7 is standing
8 is playing

2
1 have to, don't have to
2 have to, don't have to
3 doesn't have to, has to
4 doesn't have to, has to
5 have to, don't have to
6 have to, don't have to

Reading

1
1 T
2 F
3 T
4 T
5 T
6 F

3 Different styles

Unit summary

Active vocabulary

- physical appearance: height - short, tall; hair - curly, dark, light, long, straight, wavy
- clothes: boots, jacket, jeans, pants, shirt, shoes, skirt, T-shirt
- adjectives to describe clothes:, high, loose, low, tight
- personality: competitive, creative, disorganised, helpful, sociable, talkative
- nouns: organization, (identical) twins
- adjectives: big, clean, colorful, complicated, crowded, dangerous, expensive, fast, fat, identical, nervous, simple, tiring
- verbs: compete, help

Passive vocabulary

- nouns: action hero, alien, backpack, castle, fairy tale character, flower, freedom, grunge, hairstyle, lies, makeup, mess, pattern, personality, poetry, smile, stone, stranger, style, weightlifter
- verb: express, locate, point, tell lies
- adjectives: artistic, bizarre, fashionable, helpful, honest, identical, natural

Grammar

- short comparative adjectives
- long comparative adjectives

Skills

- Reading a comparison of best friends' appearance and personality
- Reading descriptions of people's personalities
- Reading an article about different styles
- Listening to a conversation about appearances
- Writing a description of a favorite person

Cross-curricular

- art and design, music

Values

- Respecting that others are different

Introducing the topic

Vocabulary

> **Aims**
> Present and practice adjectives to describe physical appearance
> Personalization of description vocabulary

Warm-up

Books closed. What styles of clothes are fashionable at the moment, e.g. tight jeans or loose jeans? What hairstyles are fashionable at the moment? Who dresses fashionably in the class? Who has got a fashionable haircut?

1 Presentation of vocabulary set: short comparative adjectives

- Look at the pictures.
- Fill in the blanks with the adjectives in the box.
- Listen, check and repeat.

🎧 **Answers / Audio CD 1 Track 16**

1	short	6	low
2	straight	7	tall
3	loose	8	wavy
4	curly	9	tight
5	long	10	high

Recycling

2 Personalization; review further practice of adjectives to describe physical appearance

- Fill in the blanks with information about you using the adjectives in exercise 1.

Answers
Students' own answers

Extend your vocabulary (Workbook page 12)

> ➡ **Workbook page 12**

Exploring the topic

Aims
Read a comparison of best friends' appearance and personality
Exposure to comparative adjectives

Reading

 Audio CD 1 track 17

Warm-up

Books closed. Has anyone got a best friend? Do they have similar personalities and like similar things to you? What are their differences?

1 **General comprehension**

• Look at the photos and read the titles.
• Answer the question.

Answers
They are best friends.

2 **General comprehension (first reading); exposure to comparative adjectives**

• Read the text quickly.
• Match the photos to the names of the friends.

Answers
Photo 1: Kara
Photo 2: Tanya

3 **Detailed comprehension task (second reading)**

• Read the statements.
• Read and listen to the text again and circle *T* (True) or *F* (False).

Answers

1	T	4	F
2	F	5	T
3	T	6	F

Grammar

Aims

Present and practice short comparative adjectives
Talk about differences

1 Grammar chart: short comparative adjectives

> **Note:**
> - We compare two or more things using the comparative form of adjectives + than.
> - We form comparatives of short adjectives by adding -er (see *Take note!*)
>
> See Grammar summary page 114.

Take note!

Spelling rules for short comparative adjectives

We make short comparative adjectives:
- of most adjectives by adding -er,
  e.g. *tight* ➡ *tighter*
- of adjectives that end in -e, by adding -r,
  e.g. *loose* ➡ *looser*
- of adjectives that end in -y, by replacing the *y* with -ier, e.g. *wavy* ➡ *wavier*
- of adjectives ending in one vowel + one consonant by doubling the final consonant and adding -er, e.g. *fit* ➡ *fitter*
- Some comparatives are irregular, e.g. *good* ➡ *better*, *bad* ➡ *worse*, *far* ➡ *farther*

2 Controlled practice of short comparative adjectives

- Read the sentences.
- Fill in the blanks with the comparative form of the adjectives in parentheses.

Answers			
1	shorter	4	funnier
2	bigger	5	noisier
3	looser	6	fatter

3 Further controlled practice of short comparative adjectives

- Look at the picture.
- Read the skeleton sentences.
- Write sentences using short comparative adjectives.

Answers
1 The tree is taller than the house.
2 The truck is bigger than the car.
3 The cat is cleaner than the dog.
4 The motorcycle is faster than the bus.
5 The girl is taller than the boy.
6 The girl's hair is curlier than the boy's hair.

4 Practice of identifying common mistakes with short comparative adjectives

- Read the sentences.
- Write the correct form of the mistake next to each sentence.

Answers			
1	taller	4	curlier
2	than	5	bigger
3	better	6	faster

Finished?

Fast finishers can do Puzzle 3A on page 105

Answers
Tim and Steven are taller than anyone else.
Peter is shorter than anyone else.

Over to you!

5 Personalization; oral practice of short comparative adjectives

- Think of two things that you can compare, e.g. two movies, two actors, two singers, two objects.
- Take turns to tell your partner the two things and compare the two things using a comparative adjective (see example).

➡ **Workbook page 13**

➡ **Mixed Ability Worksheets page 6**

Building the topic

Vocabulary

Warm-up

Books closed. How would students describe their personalities? Why? Do other students agree? How would they describe their teachers' personalities? Write any new words on the board.

1 **Presentation of vocabulary set: personality adjectives; exposure to long comparative adjectives**

- Look at the pictures and read the descriptions.
- Fill in the blanks with the words in the box.
- Listen, check and repeat.

Answers / Audio CD 1 track 18

1	sociable	4	disorganized
2	helpful	5	competitive
3	creative	6	talkative

2 **Further vocabulary practice**

- Read the statements.
- Read and listen to the texts.
- Write the name of the person next to each statement.

Audio CD 1 track 19

Answers

1	Andrew	4	Melinda
2	Joni	5	Adam
3	Dieter	6	Marcus

3 **Personalization of personality adjectives**

- Read the words in the exercise 1 again.
- Write the words which are important to you in a friend.

Answers
Students' own answers.

Extend your vocabulary (Workbook page 14)

➡ **Workbook page 14**

Grammar

Aims

Present and practice long comparative adjectives
Talk about differences

Cultural note

- Yorkshire is the largest county in England with a population of about 5 million. The cities of York and Leeds are in Yorkshire.
- Granada is a city in the southern Spain with a population of about 250,000.

1 Grammar chart: long comparative adjectives

> **Note:**
> - We form comparatives of long adjectives with *more* + adjective + *than*.
> - A long adjective has two or more syllables.
> - See Grammar summary page 114.

2 Controlled practice of long comparative adjectives; review of personality adjectives

- Read the skeleton sentences.
- Write sentences using *be* + long comparative adjectives.

Answers
1 Kathy is more helpful than Jim.
2 This book is more interesting than that book.
3 Maths is more difficult than geography.
4 Your jacket is more colorful than my jacket.
5 Your story is more exciting than my story.
6 My brother is more talkative than my sister.

3 Further practice of long comparative adjectives; revision of adjectives

- Read the information about Richmond Castle and the Alhambra.
- Fill in the blanks with the comparative form of the adjectives in parentheses + *than*.

Answers
1 more crowded than
2 older than
3 more colorful than
4 more expensive than
5 more complicated than
6 more simple than

4 Further practice of comparative adjectives

- Look at the chart.
- Write sentences about skiing and running using the comparative form of the adjectives in the chart.

Answers
1 Skiing is more expensive than running.
2 Skiing is more exciting than running.
3 Running is more tiring than skiing.
4 Skiing is more dangerous than running.
5 Skiing is more difficult than running.
6 Running is more boring than skiing.

Finished?

Fast finishers can do Puzzle 3B on page 105.

Answers

CREATIVE   COMPETATIVE
TALKATIVE   HELPFUL

SALLY IS SOCIABLE

Extra activity (all classes)

Practice short and long comparative adjectives; review vocabulary

- Write a group of words from a recently studied vocabulary set in a circle on the board, e.g. *running, playing soccer, scuba diving, painting, playing in a band, acting, working on a computer, shopping*
- Students make a sentence to compare two things, e.g. *Playing soccer is more interesting than working on a computer.*
- Draw a line between the two things that were compared.
- Ask students to make another comparison and continue until each word has at least one line connecting it to another word.
- Point to a line between two words and see if students can remember the sentence. Then delete the line.
- Continue until there are no lines.
- Stronger classes can write their own word circles and work in groups to practice comparatives.

Over to you!

5 Personalization; oral practice of long and short comparative adjectives

- Think of two activities that you can compare.
- Take turns to tell your partner the two activities and compare them using a comparative adjective (see example).

➡ **Workbook page 15**

➡ **Mixed Ability Worksheets page 7**

Living English

Aims

Read about different styles
Listen to a comparative description of teenagers
Practice listening for key words
Read a description of a favorite person
Use a chart to plan your writing
Write a description of a favourite person

Reading

 Audio CD 1 track 20

Cultural note

- **Hip hop** is a culture mainly developed by African Americans and Latinos. The culture has a distinctive style of clothing and music. Hip hop music appeared in the 1970s and became a significant part of modern music culture during the 1980s. It is now one of the best-selling types of music in the world.
- **Japanese Street** is a style mainly present in large cities such as Tokyo. The styles are unique and do not copy popular fashions.
- **Grunge** describes a style and a type of music inspired by punk, heavy metal and indie fashions and music.
- **Punk** is a style and type of music first developed in the 1970s. It was originally intended to be as shocking and rebellious as possible.
- **Hippy** refers to a 1960s culture that began in North America. At that time hippies were against middle-class values and the Vietnam War.

Warm-up

Books closed. What styles are fashionable at the moment? What are their names? Do they have special types of clothes, music or something else? Do students like the styles? What styles were fashionable five years ago? Did they like them?

Before you read

 1 Pre-reading task

- Look at the pictures.
- Answer the questions.

Answers
Students' own answers

While you read

2 General comprehension (first reading)

- Look at the photos.
- Read the article quickly.
- Write the number of the photo next to each style.

Answers
Japanese Street 1
Grunge 2
Hip hop 3
Punk 4
Hippy 5

After you read

3 Detailed comprehension (second reading)

- Read the sentences.
- Read the article again.
- Write the name(s) of the style(s) next to each sentence.

Answers
1 Hip hop, Grunge, Punk
2 Punk
3 Hip hop
4 Hippie
5 Japanese street, Punk
6 Grunge

Listening

1 Presentation and practice of listening skill (first listening)

- Read the Listening skills box.

> **Listening skills: Listening for key words**
> Listening for key words, e.g. nouns, verbs or adjectives, helps you understand the main content of a listening and answer questions.

- Read the list of adjectives.
- Listen to the conversation and check (✓) the adjectives you hear.

🎧 **Audio CD 1 track 21**

Bob: Hi, Tina. What's going on?
Tina: Amelia and I are going to a concert tonight.
Bob: Who's Amelia?
Tina: You know. She's in our class!
Bob: What does she look like?
Tina: Well ... her hair is longer than mine. And it's darker, too.
Bob: Is she really short?
Tina: No, she isn't. She's a lot taller than me, actually.
Bob: And she wears really loose jeans, right?
Tina: Well, they're looser than my jeans.
Bob: Does she wear really colorful jackets?
Tina: Yeah, that's right. All her clothes are colorful. They aren't dark like my clothes.
Bob: And she carries a really big backpack, right?
Tina: Uh...yeah, she does. It's a lot bigger than my backpack, anyway.
Bob: Oh – I know who she is. She's cute!

Answers

1	longer	5	looser
2	darker	7	colorful
3	taller	8	bigger

2 Detailed comprehension of listening text (second listening)

- Read the sentences.
- Listen again and circle the correct words.

Answers

1	longer	4	more colorful
2	taller	5	bigger
3	looser		

Writing

1 General comprehension of writing model

- Read the questions.
- Read the text, looking for key words, e.g. names and personality adjectives.
- Answer the questions.

Answers

His favorite person is his brother Carlos.
He's very sociable, honest and helpful.

2 Detailed comprehension of writing model

- Read the text again.
- Fill in the chart with information about Carlos

Answers

Name	Carlos
Age	18
Appearance	tall, strong, short hair, fashionable, looks good
Personality	sociable (loves going to parties and going out with his friends), honest (never tells lies), helpful (always does good things for people – with a smile)

3 Preparation for personalized writing

- Copy the chart in exercise 2 and fill it in with information about your favourite person's name, age, appearance and personality.

4 Personalized writing

- Follow the writing model and use the chart in exercise 3.
- Write about your favorite person.

➡ Tests page 6

3 Review

Vocabulary

1
1. straight
2. short
3. tight
4. low
5. wavy
6. curly
7. long
8. loose
9. high

2
1. creative
2. disorganized
3. sociable
4. talkative
5. competitive
6. helpful

Grammar

1
1. taller than
2. longer than
3. shorter than
4. tighter than
5. looser
6. happier

2
1. more amazing than
2. better than
3. more competitive than
4. colder than
5. more difficult than
6. more nervous than
7. happier than

Study skills

1
1. organized
2. organization
3. compete
4. competitive
5. help
6. helpful

4 On vacation

Unit summary

Active vocabulary

- weather: hot, warm, cold, cloudy, rainy, windy, sunny, snowy, icy
- Seasons: spring, summer, fall, winter
- holiday problems: fall, break, sprain, hurt, slip, feel sick, get blisters, faint,

Passive vocabulary

- nouns: accident, adrenaline, ankle, aquarium, Arctic circle, backpack, campsite, case, connection, dance group, daylight, dolphin, dose, equipment, Eskimo, exhibit, fjords, French fries, humidity, hurricane, igloo, injury, lion, marine life, must-see, octopus, patient, penguin, pressure, reactions, reflexes, relation, (religious) image, scenery, seal, shark, ski instructor, ski resort, sky, snow storm, snowball, snow boots, snowmobile, snow sled, spirits, stars, statue, temple, tour guide, tower, transportation, weather conditions, whale
- adjectives: active, awesome, Balinese, bright, cute, embarrassing, energetic, fascinating, impressive, interactive, Norwegian, perfect, reclining, scared, stormy
- verbs: dare, go rafting, go trekking, guess, make something (hurt), observe, prove, show, slip
- other: full of, indoor, on top of, outside, scientifically

Grammar

- *was / were*
- simple past (affirmative)

Skills

- Reading a travel diary
- Reading a text about how the weather affects people
- Listening to an interview about the lifestyle of Eskimos
- Asking about vacations in the past
- Pronunciation of /d/ and /ð/ sounds.

Cross-curricular

- geography

Values

- health

Introducing the topic

Vocabulary

> **Aims**
> Present and practice weather vocabulary
> Personalization of weather vocabulary

Warm-up

Books closed. What's the weather like today? What was it like yesterday? How do students feel when they see rain, sun, etc.? Has anyone / everyone in the class seen snow?

1 Presentation of vocabulary set: weather

- Look at the picture.
- Label the weather symbols with the words in the box.
- Listen, check and repeat.

🎧 **Answers / Audio CD 1 track 22**

1	cloudy	6	hot
2	rainy	7	icy
3	windy	8	snowy
4	warm	9	cold
5	sunny		

Recycling

2 Personalization; vocabulary practice; review seasons

- Look at the pictures and read the texts.
- Write the weather word(s) next to each season for where you live.

Answers
Students' own answers

Extend your vocabulary (Workbook page 16)

> ➡ **Workbook page 16**

Exploring the topic

Reading

 Audio CD 1 track 23

Cultural note

- **Nepal** is a country in Asia. Its capital is Kathmandu and its population is 28 million. The most-spoken language is Nepali.
- **Laos** is a country in south-east Asia. Its capital is Vientiane and it's population is 6 million. The official language is Lao.
- **Indonesia** is a country of over 17,500 islands in south-east Asia. About 6,000 of the islands are inhabited. Its capital is Jakarta and its population is 245 million. The official language is Bahasa Indonesian.

Warm-up

Have students heard of or been to any of the places in the text? Have they ever written a travel diary about places they have been to?

1 **General comprehension (first reading); exposure to *was / were***

- Look at the attractions of the countries.
- Read the text quickly and match the places to the attractions.

Answers
1	c	3	b
2	a		

2 **General comprehension (second reading)**

- Read and listen to the text.
- Fill in the blanks with the names of the places.

Answers
1	Indonesia	2	Nepal, Laos

3 **Detailed comprehension (third reading); review of weather vocabulary**

- Read the sentences about the weather
- Read the text again and fill in the blanks with the correct weather.

Answers
1	snowy, icy, cold	3	hot, sunny, windy
2	rainy, sunny		

Grammar

Aims
Review and practice simple past *be* and *there was / there were* (affirmative, negative and questions)

1 Grammar chart: simple past *be* and *there was / there were* (affirmative and negative)

Note:
- The affirmative past form of *be* is *was / were*.
- The negative past form of *be* is *wasn't* (= was not) / *weren't* (= were not).
- We use:
  - *there was / wasn't* to talk about singular nouns in the past, e.g. *There was a beach.*
  - *there were / weren't* to talk about plural nouns in the past, e.g. *There were some tourists.*
- See Grammar summary page 114.

2 Controlled practice of *was / were*

- Read the sentences.
- Circle the correct form of the verb.

Answers
1 was   2 were   3 was   4 were
5 was   6 were

3 Controlled practice of *there was / there were*

- Look at the picture about New Zealand.
- Read the sentences.
- Fill in the blanks with *There was / were, There wasn't / weren't*.

Answers
1 There were   2 There were   3 There wasn't
4 There weren't   5 There was

4 Grammar chart: simple past *be* and *there was / there were* (questions)

Note:
- We make questions in the simple past *be* by swapping the verb and the subject, e.g. *Were you in Europe last year?*
- We make short answers with *Yes / No,* + subject + *was / wasn't / were / weren't*.
- We make questions with *there was / there were* by swapping the order of *there* and the verb *be*, e.g. *Were there any mountains?*
- We make short answers with *Yes, / No,* + *there + was / wasn't / were / weren't*.
- We use questions with *What ... like?* to ask about the nature of people or things, e.g. *What was the weather like? It was sunny.*
- See Grammar summary page 114.

5 Further controlled practice of simple past (questions)

- Read the skeleton sentences.
- Write questions in the simple past *be*.

Answers
Were you in Africa on your vacation?
What was the weather like?
When were you there?
Was Kasia with you?
Were there any special attractions?

6 Further controlled practice of simple past (questions and answers)

- Read the questions in exercise 5 again.
- Read the answers.
- Write the number of the correct question next to each answer.

Answers
1 3   2 1   3 5   4 2   5 4

Finished?
Fast finishers can do Puzzle 4A on page 107.

Answers
vxqqb = sunny	udiqb = rainy
vqrzb = snowy	ziqgb = windy
forxgb = cloudy	ifb = icy

Over to you!

7 Personalization; written practice of past simple *be* and *there was / there were* (affirmative)

- Write a description of an amazing place you went on vacation.
- Invent information if you want.
- Use the writing model to help you.

➡ **Workbook page 17**

➡ **Mixed Ability Worksheets page 8**

Building the topic

Vocabulary

> ### Aims
> Present and practice holiday problems
> Model simple past regular and irregular (affirmative)
> Model time phrases used with the simple past

Cultural note

- **Miami Beach** is a city in the state of Florida in the USA. It is a popular holiday destination.
- **Denmark** is a country in Europe. Its capital is Copenhagen and its population is 5.5 million. It is part of Scandinavia.
- **Chile** is a country in South America. Its capital is Santiago and its population is 16.5 million. The official language is Spanish. It is one of the longest countries in the world.
- **Montana** is the fourth largest state in the USA. Its population is one million. It has one of the smallest populations in the United States.
- **Florida** is a state in the south-east of the USA. Its population is 18 million. It has some of the severest weather in the United States.
- **Colorado** is a state in the west of the USA. Its population is about 5 million. In this state the plains meet the Rockies.

Warm-up

Books closed. Where did students last go on vacation? Did they have any problems? What happened?

1 Presentation of vocabulary set: holiday problems

- Look at the pictures.
- Write the correct number of the picture next to each verb.
- Listen, check and repeat.

🎧 **Answers / Audio CD 1 track 24**

1	sprain	5	faint
2	feel sick	6	get blisters
3	slip		
4	hurt		

2 Vocabulary practice; detailed comprehension

- Read the statements
- Read and listen to the text.
- Write the correct name next to each statement.

🎧 **Audio CD 1 track 25**

Answers

1	Kylie	4	Antonio
2	Alex	5	Javier
3	Olivia	6	Katherine

Extra activity (all classes)

Further practice of reading text

- Write the questions on the board.
- Students read the text again and write the answers.
  1. How many blisters did Olivia get?
  2. Who was really cute?
  3. Who is not very active?
  4. Why did Javier slip?
  5. Who was with friends on holiday?

Answers

1. Eight
2. Kylie's tour guide
3. Olivia
4. Because the mountain was icy.
5. Alex

Extend your vocabulary (Workbook page 18)

> ➡ **Workbook page 18**

Grammar

Aims

Present and practice simple past regular and irregular (affirmative)
Present and practice spelling rules for regular simple past verbs
Talk about the past

Cultural note

- **Norway** is a country in the north of Europe. Its capital is Oslo. It is part of Scandinavia and famous for its fjords.

1 Grammar chart: simple past regular and irregular (affirmative)

Note:
- We use the simple past to talk about actions that started and finished in the past.
- Regular verbs end in -ed. (see *Take note!* below)
- Irregular verbs have their own past forms, e.g. *feel* ➡ *felt*.
- The simple past form of verbs is the same for all persons, e.g. *I / you* (singular) / *he / she / it / you* (plural) / *they slipped*.
- For the spelling rules of simple past regular forms, see *Take note!* (below).
- See Grammar summary page 114.

Take note!

Spelling rules
- The simple past of regular verbs ending is -ed, e.g. *travel* ➡ *traveled*. We make the simple past of verbs:
  – ending in -e by adding -d, e.g. *arrive* ➡ *arrived*
  – ending in one vowel + one consonant by doubling the final consonant and adding -ed, e.g. *slip* ➡ *slipped*. Common exceptions to this rule are words ending in -l, e.g. *travel* ➡ *traveled*.
  – ending in a consonant and *y* by replacing the *y* with *i* and adding -ed, e.g. *carry* ➡ *carried*
- There are no spelling rules for irregular verbs.

2 Controlled practice of simple past (affirmative) regular verbs

- Read the sentences.
- Fill in the blanks with the simple past of the verbs in parentheses.

Answers

1	traveled	4	arrived	7	danced
2	carried	5	toured		
3	waited	6	surfed		

3 Further controlled practice of simple past (affirmative) regular and irregular verbs

- Read the diary.
- Fill in the blanks with the simple past of the verbs in parentheses.
- Use the irregular verb list on page 120 if necessary.

Answers

1	met	4	went	7	fell
2	stayed	5	climbed	8	celebrated
3	had	6	slipped		

Finished?

Fast finishers can do Puzzle 4B on page 107.

Answers
I HURT MY KNEE
MOM GOT BLISTERS.
DAD FELT SICK.
LISA BROKE HER LEG.

Over to you!

4 Personalization; oral practice of simple past (affirmative) and holiday problems vocabulary

- Write three sentences about problems you had on vacation. Use your imagination if you want.
- Take turns to read a sentence to the class.
- Students guess how the problem happened (see example).

➡ **Workbook page 19**

➡ **Mixed Ability Worksheets page 9**

Living English

Aims
Read about how the weather affects your body, feelings and mind
Listen to an interview about the life of Eskimos
Talk about your vacation
Use the /d/ and /ð/ sounds accurately

Reading

 Audio CD 1 track 26

Warm up!

Books closed. How are the students feeling today? Is the weather affecting them? Do they feel different in different weather conditions?

Cultural note

- **Hippocrates** (470 BC–370 BC), also known as the "Father of Medicine" was an ancient Greek physician. He was the first physician to believe that diseases were not the punishment of gods but due to environmental, diet and lifestyles.

Before you read

1 **Pre-reading task**

- Read and answer the questions.

Answers
Students' own answers

While you read

2 **Presentation and practice of reading skill; general comprehension (first reading)**

- Read the Reading skills box.

> **Reading skills: Getting the general idea**
> - When you read a text for the first time, it helps to read it quickly to get the general idea. You do not need to understand every word. When you read the text a second time, you will already have an idea of what the content is. This can be a useful technique in exams.

- Read the facts.
- Read the each paragraph of the text quickly.
- Write the number of the paragraph next to each heading.

Answers

1	Paragraph 3	3	Paragraph 1
2	Paragraph 4	4	Paragraph 2

After you read

3 **Detailed comprehension (second reading)**

- Read the statements.
- Read the text again.
- Circle *T* (True) or *F* (False).

Answers

1	T	3	F	5	T
2	T	4	F	6	F

Listening

Cultural note

- **Alaska** is a state in the north-west of the USA. It is connected to Canada. It is the largest state but has one of the smallest populations of 650,000.
- **Canada** is a country north of the USA. It is the second largest country in the world. It is a member of the British Commonwealth. Its capital is Ottawa.
- **Greenland** is a country which is part of Denmark but it has its own government. Its capital is Nuuk.
- **Iceland** see page 18, Exploring the topic.

1 Pre-listening task

- Look at the photos.
- Write a word in the box below each photo.

Answers
1 snowmobile   3 Eskimo   2 snowsled

2 General comprehension of listening text (first listening)

- Read the words.
- Listen and check (✔) the topics they talk about.

 **Audio CD 1 track 27**

Daniel is a journalist. He's interviewing a scientist, Samuel Brooks. He's asking questions about Eskimos' life in the past and nowadays.

Daniel:	Where do Eskimos live?
Samuel:	They live in the Arctic Circle, in Alaska, Canada and Greenland.
Daniel:	What's the weather like in the Arctic Circle?
Samuel:	Very cold! From zero to minus 70 degrees.
Daniel:	In the past, what did Eskimos wear?
Samuel:	They wore animal furs.
Daniel:	And, where did they live?
Samuel:	They lived in igloos. Igloos are houses made of snow.
Daniel:	What did Eskimos eat?
Samuel:	They ate a lot of fish and meat. They didn't eat many vegetables.
Daniel:	How did they travel?
Samuel:	They traveled by dog sled.
Daniel:	How do Eskimos live nowadays?
Samuel:	Eskimos have a modern life. They wear regular clothes and travel by snowmobile.
Daniel:	Thanks Samuel.

Answers
weather, houses, food, clothes, transportation

3 Detailed comprehension of listening text (second listening)

- Read the sentences and the possible answers.
- Listen again and circle a or b.

Answers
1 a   2 b   3 b   5 a   4 a

Speaking

1 First listening

- Look at the pictures and read the model dialogs.
- Listen and read.

 **Audio CD 1 track 28**

2 Presentation of pronunciation point

> **Pronunciation: /d/ and /ð/**
> - The /d/ and /ð/ sounds can be confused.
> - Read the example words.
> - Listen and repeat, copying /d/ and /ð/.

 **Audio CD 1 track 29**

3 Pronunciation practice

- Read the words in the box.
- Listen and write the words in the correct column.

 **Audio CD 1 track 30**

Answers

/d/	/ð/
Dan	than
dose	those
dare	there

4 Dialog practice

- Practice the model dialogs with another student.
- Change roles and practice again.

5 Dialog personalization and practice

- Look at the words in blue in the model dialog.
- Think of some different situations.
- Replace the blue words with your ideas to make a new dialog.
- Practice the dialog with another student.

➡ Tests page 8

4 Review

Vocabulary

1 1 cloudy
   2 hot
   3 rainy
   4 cold
   5 sunny
   6 snowy
   7 warm
   8 icy

2 1 sprained
   2 felt sick
   3 got blisters
   4 hurt
   5 fainted
   6 slipped

Grammar

1 1 were
   2 were
   3 was
   4 were
   5 was
   6 were

2 1 started
   2 fell
   3 went
   4 bought
   5 had
   6 visited
   7 played
   8 threw

Reading

1 1 T
   2 T
   3 F
   4 T
   5 F

Music world

Unit summary

Active vocabulary

- musical instruments: bass, drums, guitar, keyboard, microphone, piano
- musicians: bass guitarist, drummer, guitarists, keyboard player, pianist
- biography verbs: become famous, grow up, have a hit record, record an album, sign a contract, start her career, was born, win an award

Grammar

- simple past (*yes / no* questions and negatives)
- simple past (*wh-* questions)

Skills

- Reading about legendary and contemporary bands
- Reading the history of a virtual band
- Writing a biography
- Talking about what you did in the past
- Using appropriate intonation in questions

Cross-curricular

- music, history

Values

- recognizing the importance of individuality

Introducing the topic

Vocabulary

> **Aims**
>
> Present and practice musical instruments
> Personalization of music vocabulary

Cultural note

- **Stacey Ferguson** is a member of the Black Eyed Peas, an American hip-hop band. They were formed in 1995 and their most successful records include *Elephunk* (2003) and *Monkey Business* (2005).
- **The Edge** is a member of U2, an Irish rock band. They were formed in 1976 and have consistently been one of the most popular bands in the world. Their most successful records include *The Joshua Tree* (1986) and *Achtung Baby* (1991).
- **Garry Berryson** is a member of Coldplay, an alternative rock band from England. They formed in 1998 and their most successful records include *Parachutes* (2000) and *A Rush of Blood to the Head* (2002).
- **Tré Cool** is a member of Green Day, an American punk rock band. They formed in 1989. Their successful records include *Dookie* (1994) and *American Idiot* (2004).
- **Jonny Greenwood** is a member of Radiohead, a rock band from Oxford in England. They formed in 1986. Their successful records include *The Bends* (1995) and *OK Computer* (1997).
- **Alicia Keys** is an American R&B singer and songwriter. Her most successful records include *Songs in A Minor* (2001) and *The Diary of Alicia Keys* (2003).

Warm-up

Look at the photos of the different bands and singers. Have students got any music by the artists? Which is their favourite band or singer of those in the photos?

1 **Presentation of vocabulary set: musical instruments**

- Look at the photos.
- Write the number of a photo next to each word.
- Listen, check and repeat.

🎧 **Answers / Audio CD 1 track 31**

| 1 microphone | 2 bass | 3 piano |
| 4 drums | 5 keyboard | 6 guitar |

Recycling

2 **Practice and review types of musician**

- Look at the photos again.
- Fill in the blanks with the correct names from the photos and the instruments in exercise 1.

Answers

1 Stacey Ferguson	4 Johnny Greenwood
2 The Edge	5 Guy Berryman
3 Tré Cool	6 Alicia Keys

Extend your vocabulary (Workbook page 20)

> ➡ Workbook page 20

Exploring the topic

Aims

Read about legends and contemporary bands
Model simple past (questions and short answers)
Review simple past (affirmative and negative)

Reading

 **Audio CD 1 track 32**

Cultural note

- **Red Hot Chilli Peppers** are an American rock band which formed in 1984. They fuse different types of music.
- **The Killers** are an American rock / indie band from Nevada. They formed in 2002 and have had international success.
- **Ozzy Osborne** (born December 3, 1948) is an English singer. He was the lead singer of the heavy metal band *Black Sabbath*. Between 2002 and 2005 Ozzy appeared on a reality TV show on MTV about his family called *The Osbornes*.
- **Led Zeppelin** were an English rock band and one of the most successful bands in popular music history. They formed in 1968 and split up in 1980. To date, the band has sold more than 300 million albums around the world.
- **The Clash** were an English punk rock band. They formed in 1976 and split up in 1986. Their most successful record was *London Calling* (1979), which is considered by many critics to be one of the greatest albums in the history of rock music.
- **Joss Stone** (born April 11, 1987) is an English soul singer and songwriter. Her most successful record is *The Soul Sessions* (2003), which she released when she was only 16.
- **Beyoncé** (born September 4, 1981) is an American R&B singer and songwriter. She is also part of the band *Destiny's Child*, who formed in 1990 when Beyoncé was only nine years old.
- **Aretha Franklin** (born March 25, 1942) is an American soul singer who is often called "The Queen of Soul". She has had 17 top ten records in America and has won 18 Grammy awards in the USA for her music and achievements.
- **Snoop Dogg** (born October 20, 1971) is an American rap singer, songwriter and actor.
- **Eminem** (born Marshall Bruce Mathers III, October 17, 1972) is an American rap singer and songwriter.
- **The Fatback Band** are an American funk band which formed in 1973 and were most successful in the 1970s and 1980s.

Warm-up

Books closed. What kind of music do the students' parents listen to? Do they listen to contemporary music or bands from when they were young? Do students like any of the music their parents listen to?

1 Detailed comprehension (first reading); exposure to simple past (yes/no questions)

- Read the statements.
- Read the text.
- Circle *T* (True) or *F* (False).

Answers

1	F	4	T
2	T	5	F
3	F		

2 Detailed comprehension (second reading)

- Look at the chart.
- Read and listen to the text.
- Fill in the gaps with the missing music styles, contemporary bands / singers and legendary bands.

Answers

1 Heavy Metal
2 Led Zeppelin / Black Sabbath
3 Green Day
4 The Class
5 Soul
6 Aretha Franklin
7 Rap
8 Snoop Dogg / Eminem

Grammar

Aims
Present and practice the simple past (*yes / no* questions and short answers)
Ask and answer about the past
Present and practice the simple past (negative)
Talk about the past

1 Grammar chart: simple past (*yes / no* questions and short answers)

Note:
- We form the simple past (*yes / no* questions) with *Did* + subject pronoun + verb, e.g. *Did you go?* NOT ~~Did you went?~~ We make short answers with *did* only NOT with the main verb e.g. *Yes, I did.* NOT ~~Yes, I went~~.
- See Grammar summary page 114.

2 Controlled practice of simple past (*yes / no* questions and short answers)

- Read Green Day's fact file.
- Read the skeleton questions.
- Write *yes / no* questions.
- Use the fact file to answer the questions.

Answers
1 Did Green Day start playing in 1988?
  Yes, they did.
2 Did the band form in New York?
  No, it didn't.
3 Did the band record *Holiday* in 2004?
  No, they didn't.
4 Did the album *Dookie* sell a lot of copies?
  Yes, it did.
5 Did the band win an award in 1996?
  No, they didn't.
6 Did the band play at Woodstock in 1994?
  Yes, they did.

3 Grammar chart: simple past (negative)

Note:
- We form the simple past negative with the subject pronoun + *didn't* + verb e.g. *I didn't go.* NOT ~~I didn't went~~.
- See Grammar summary page 114.

4 Controlled practice of simple past (negative)

- Read the sentences.
- Rewrite the sentences using the simple past negative.
- Write the correct sentences using the words in parentheses.

Answers
1 He didn't play the drums. He played the guitar.
2 They didn't play punk rock. They played pop rock.
3 He didn't record *Slim Shady* in 2005. He recorded *Curtain Call*.
4 They didn't start playing in 1985. They started playing in 1999.
5 She didn't grow up in London. She grew up in New York.
6 They didn't form in 2002. They formed in 1998.

Finished?
Fast finishers can do Puzzle 5A on page 107.

Answers
1 Keyboards – Rose
2 Guitar – Tomas
3 Drums – Harvey
4 Piano – Josh
5 Bass – Lilia

Over to you!

5 Personalization; oral practice of simple past (*yes / no* questions and short answers)

- Read the list of verbs.
- Take turns to ask your partner simple past *yes / no* questions.
- Answer your partner's questions.

Extra activity (all classes)

Practice of simple past (affirmative, negative and questions)

- Ask students to imagine they were in a famous legendary band, e.g. *The Clash* or *The Rolling Stones*.
- In groups, students take turn to ask *yes / no* questions to the person, e.g. *Did you play the guitar? Did your group play rock music?*
- Students try to guess which band the others were in.

➡ **Workbook page 21**

➡ **Mixed Ability Worksheets page 10**

Building the topic

Vocabulary

Aims
Present and practice biography verbs
Model simple past (*wh-* questions)
Review simple past (affirmative)

Cultural note
- **Joss Stone** see page 42, Reading.
- **Shakira** (born February 2, 1977) is a Colombian pop singer and songwriter. She is the highest-selling Colombian artist of all time and the only Colombian artist to have had a number one single in the USA.
- **Colombia** is a country in South America. Its capital is Bogotá and its population is 44 million. Its official language is Spanish.
- **The Grammy Awards** or "Grammies" are annual music awards in the USA.

Warm-up
Look at the photo. Have students heard of Joss Stone? What kind of music do they think she sings? How old do they think she is?

1 Presentation of vocabulary set: biography verbs

- Read the text about Joss Stone.
- Fill in the blanks in the questions with the verb phrases in the box.
- Listen, check and repeat.

 **Answers / Audio CD 1 track 33**

A was born	E record an album
B grow up	F become famous
C start her career	G have a hit record.
D sign a contract	H win an award

2 Vocabulary practice; exposure to simple past (*wh-* questions) and answers

- Read and listen to the text.
- Listen again and repeat the questions.

 **Audio CD 1 track 34**

3 Further exposure to simple past (*wh-* questions) and answers.

- Read the sentences about Shakira.
- Write the letter of the question from the text about Joss Stone next to each answer.

Answers

1	C	5	G
2	E	6	A
3	B	7	F
4	H	8	D

Extra activity (stronger classes)

Practice of simple past (affirmative, negative and *Wh-* questions)

- Students use the text about Joss Stone to write questions and answers about one of their favourite singers.
- Students can add more questions to the interview.

Extend your vocabulary (Workbook page 22)

➡ **Workbook page 22**

Grammar

1 Grammar chart: simple past (*wh-* questions)

Note:

- We form *wh-* questions in the simple past by adding the *wh- word* to the beginning of the *yes / no* question, e.g. *Why did you go?*
- *What* asks about things.
- *Where* asks about places.
- *When* asks about a time or date.
- *Why* asks about reasons.
- *How* asks about the manner or way.
- *How many* asks about the quantity.
- See Grammar summary page 115.

2 Controlled practice of *wh-* question words

- Read the *wh-* questions.
- Circle the correct question word in each question.

Answers

1	Who	4	How
2	When	5	What
3	Where	6	What

3 Controlled practice of simple past (*wh-* questions)

- Read the profile of Beyoncé.
- Read the skeleton questions.
- Write *wh-* questions.

Answers

1 When was she born?
2 Where did she start singing?
3 What did Destiny's Child record their first album?
4 How many albums did Destiny's Child sell?
5 When did Destiny's Child win an MTV Award?

4 Further practice of simple past (*wh-* questions) and answers.

- Read the profile of Beyoncé again and the answers A–E.
- Write the number of a question from exercise 3 next to each answer.

Answers

A	4	D	3
B	5	E	2
C	1		

5 Controlled practice of simple past (*wh-* questions)

- Read the answers about Beyoncé.
- Write questions with *When did she first / last ... ?* for each answer.

Answers

1 When did she first act?
2 When did she first sing?
3 When did she last record with Destiny's child?
4 When did she first record?

Finished?

Fast finishers can do Puzzle 5B on page 107

Answers
formed
started
recorded
signed
became

Over to you!

6 Personalization; oral practice of simple past (*When did you first / last ... ?*)

- Read the list of verb phrases.
- Take turns to ask your partner simple past questions with *When did you first / last ... ?*
- Answer your partner's questions.

→ **Workbook page 23**

→ **Mixed Ability Worksheets page 11**

Living English

Aims

Read the biography of a virtual band
Practice past time expressions
Use a chart to plan your writing
Ask and answer about what you did in the past
Use appropriate intonation in *yes / no* and *wh-*
questions

Reading

 Audio CD 1 track 35

Cultural note

- **The Archies** were the first virtual band to appear in
  worldwide pop charts. In 1969, The Monkees wrote
  Sugar Sugar, and performed it to their manager. He
  took the song and created a band based on a
  popular comic book.

Warm-up

Do students recognize the cartoon characters? Have
they heard of the band Gorillaz? Do they know any of
their songs?

Before you read

1 **Pre-reading task**

- Look at the picture.
- Answer the question.

Answer
Students' own answers

While you read

2 **General comprehension (first reading)**

- Read the beginnings and ends of the sentences.
- Read the text.
- Match the beginnings 1–4 with the endings A–D.

Answers

1	C	3	B
2	D	4	A

After you read

3 **Detailed comprehension (second reading)**

- Read the events.
- Read the text again.
- Write a number next to each event in the order
  they happen in the history of Gorillaz.

Answers
1 Murdoc hurt 2D's eye in a music store.
2 Murdoc took care of 2D.
3 Murdoc found the drummer, Russel, in a rap store.
4 Noodle, the guitarist, came in a packet from
  Japan.
5 The band gave a concert
6 The band signed a contract.
7 Gorillaz recorded their first album.

Extra activity (all classes)

Practice of simple past (affirmative, negative)

- Ask students to invent their own virtual band.
- Students write a list of the members and the
  instruments they play.
- Students add the story of how they met and their
  first record deal.

Writing

1 Presentation of writing skill

- Read the Writing skills box.

> **Writing skills: Dates and time expressions**
> Using dates and time expressions in some texts adds important details to your writing and makes it more interesting.

2 Practice of writing skill

- Read Damon Albarn's biography.
- Circle the dates and time expressions.

Answers

March 23rd, 1968	in 1987
when he was twelve	A year later
After high school	in 1999

3 Detailed analysis of writing model

- Look at the chart.
- Read the biography again.
- Complete the chart with the events in Damon Albarn's biography.

Answers

Singer	Date and time expressions	Event
Damon Albarn	March 23rd, 1968	was born
	when he was twelve	started playing violin and the piano
	After high school	studied drama
	in 1987	went to London
	A year later	formed a band, Circus
	in 1999	formed Gorillaz

4 Preparation for personalized writing

- Find information about one of your favorite singers.
- Fill in the chart with dates / time expressions and events from his / her life.

5 Personalized writing

- Follow the writing model.
- Use the information from the chart in exercise 4.
- Write a biography of one of your favorite singers.

Speaking

1 First listening

- Look at the pictures and read the model dialogs.
- Listen and read.

🎧 Audio CD 1 track 36

2 Presentation of pronunciation point

> **Pronunciation: Intonation**
> - When you ask *yes / no* questions your voice goes up. When you ask *wh-* questions your voice goes down.
> - Read the example questions.
> - Listen and repeat, copying the intonation.

🎧 Audio CD 1 track 37

3 Pronunciation practice

- Read the questions.
- Write ↗ or ↘ at the end of each sentence.
- Listen, check and repeat

🎧 Answers / Audio CD 1 track 38

1 ↘		3 ↗	
2 ↗		4 ↘	

4 Dialog practice

- Practice the model dialogs with another student.
- Change roles and practice again.

5 Dialog personalization and practice

- Look at the words in blue in the model dialog.
- Think of some different activities and what you thought of them.
- Replace the blue words with your ideas to make a new dialog.
- Practice the dialog with another student.

➡ Tests page 10

5 Review

Vocabulary 5

1
1 microphone
2 drums
3 bass
4 guitar
5 keyboards
6 piano

2
1 was born
2 grew up
3 started her career
4 signed a contract
5 became famous
6 won

Grammar

1
1 Did she grow up, Yes, she did
2 Did she start her career, No, she didn't
3 Did she sign a contract, Yes, she did
4 Did she become famous, Yes, she did
5 Did she win an award, No, she didn't

2
1 was he born
2 was he born
3 did he start his career
4 did he grow up
5 did he become famous
6 did he win an award

Study skills

1
1 song lyrics
2 stores
3 advertisments
4 signs
5 movies

2 Students' own answers

6 The coolest places

Unit summary

Active vocabulary

- describing a place: crowded, deep, large, long, narrow, small, tall, wide
- travel activities: bargain for souvenirs, buy a ticket, camp, carry your passport, drop litter, follow the rules, take a tour, use a credit card
- noun: lake

Passive vocabulary

- nouns: Antarctic, army, art scene, borders, bottled water, building, climate, floor, guard towers, parts, port, report card, runner, side steps, sights, staircase, street market, sun cream, sunburn, tap water, walker, (widest) point,
- adjectives: crowded, deep, forbidden, independent, mad, man-made, pre-school, square kilometre, unforgettable, varied, wide
- verbs: combine, follow (the rules), forget, organized, spend

- other: on your own, outdoors, whatever

Grammar

- superlative adjectives
- *have to / can't*
- *don't have to / can*

Skills

- Reading facts about places around the world
- Reading travel advice about the Great Wall of China
- Reading about places young people like to travel to
- Listening to a conversation about a new school
- Writing a brochure about a place

Cross-curricular

- geography

Values

- tolerance and respect, safety

Introducing the topic

Vocabulary

> **Aims**
>
> Present and practice adjectives to describe a place
> Personalization of description vocabulary

Cultural note

- **The Empire State Building** is a 102-story skyscraper in New York City. It was built in 1931.
- **The Nile** is a river in Africa and is the longest river on Earth.
- **The Louvre Museum** is in Paris, France, and is one of the largest and oldest art galleries and museums in the world. It holds some of the world's most famous works of art, such as Leonardo Da Vinci's *Mona Lisa.* Every year it is visited by about seven million people.
- **Lake Michigan** is one of the five Great Lakes of the USA. It is almost 500 km long and 200 km wide.

Warm-up

Look at the photos. What adjective can we use to describe the different places and things, e.g. *a long road*, *a wide road*, *a tall building*, etc.

1 Presentation of vocabulary set: describing a place

- Look at the photos.
- Read the words in the box.
- Write the number of a photo next to each word.
- Listen, check and repeat.

🎧 **Answers / Audio CD 1 track 39**

1	long	5	deep
2	wide	6	narrow
3	large	7	crowded
4	tall	8	small

Recycling

2 Personalization; further practice of adjectives to describe a place

- Read the phrases 1–4.
- Think of an example of these places in your country.

Answers

Students' own answers

Extend your vocabulary (Workbook page 24)

> ➡ **Workbook page 24**

Exploring the topic

Reading

🎧 **Audio CD 1 track 40**

Cultural note

- **Switzerland** is a country in Central Europe. Its capital is Bern and its population is 7.5 million. The official languages are German, French and Italian.
- **Taiwan** is an island nation that is part of the Republic of China.
- **Manila** is the capital of the Philippines in south-east Asia.
- **Siberia** is a large region of Russia that occupies over half of the country.
- **India** is a country in south Asia. Its capital is New Delhi and its population is 1.1 billion. The most important languages are English and Hindi.
- **Argentina** is a country in South America. Its capital is Buenos Aires and its population is 40 million. The official language is Spanish.
- **Uruguay** is a country in South America. Its capital is Montevideo and its population is 3.5 million. The official language is Spanish.

Warm-up

Look at the photos. Where do students think the places are?

1 **Pre-reading task**

- Look at the photos.
- Answer the questions.

Answers
Students' own answers

2 **General comprehension; exposure to superlative adjectives**

- Read the statements.
- Read and listen to the text.
- Write the correct letter next to each statement.

Answers

1	F	5	C
2	B	6	G
3	D	7	A
4	E		

Extra activity (stronger classes)

Practice comparative and superlative adjectives

- Ask students some quiz questions about places in the world, e.g. *Which country is the largest: Canada, China or America? (Canada) Which language is the most popular: English, Mandarin Chinese or Spanish? (Mandarin Chinese)*
- Student can write their own questions using superlative adjectives and ask and answer in groups.

Grammar

1 Grammar chart: superlative adjectives

Note:
- We form superlative sentences with:
  noun + *be* + *the* + superlative + noun
  (+ phrase), e.g. *The Nile is the longest river in the world*.
- See Grammar summary page 115.

Take note!

Spelling rules for superlative adjectives

- We make superlative adjectives:
  – of short adjectives of one syllable by adding *the* and *-est*, e.g. *long* ➡ *the longest*
  – of short adjectives that end in *-e*, by adding *the* and *-st*, e.g. *wide* ➡ *the widest*
  – of short adjectives that end in *-y*, by replacing the *y* with *-iest*, e.g. *tidy* ➡ *the tidiest*
  – of short adjectives ending in one vowel + one consonant by doubling the final consonant and adding *the* and *-est*, e.g. *big* ➡ *the biggest*
  – of long adjectives by adding *the* + *most* + the adjective.
  Some superlatives adjectives are irregular, e.g. *good* ➡ *the best*, *bad* ➡ *the worst*, *far* ➡ *the farthest*

2 Controlled practice of superlative adjectives

- Read the sentences.
- Circle the correct form of the superlative adjectives.

Answers

1	shortest	4	worst
2	most interesting	5	the fastest
3	biggest		

3 Controlled practice of superlative adjectives

- Look at the pictures.
- Fill in the blanks with the correct form of a superlative adjective in the box.

Answers

1	the tallest	4	the scariest
2	the most difficult	5	the youngest
3	the most crowded	6	the best

4 Further practice of superlative adjectives; review of comparative adjectives

- Read the sentence skeletons.
- Write sentences with the comparative or superlative form of the adjectives.

Answers
1 Jammy's is the best restaurant in our city.
2 Kelly is taller than Dawn.
3 My village is the most beautiful place in the country.
4 Jan's school is bigger than her brother's school.
5 Everest is the highest mountain in the world.
6 My MP3 player is more expensive than your DVD player.

Finished?

Fast finishers can do Puzzle 6A on page 107.

Answers
Class 6A win the award for the noisiest group, **crowdedest** (*the most crowded*), and dirtiest classroom, **annoyingest** (*most annoying*) students, **baddest** (*worst*) grammar grades and banner with **mowst** (*the most*) mistakes.

Over to you!

5 Oral practice of superlative adjectives

- Work in pairs.
- Take turns. Think of a person or place.
- Your partner makes a superlative sentence about the person or place.
- Tell your partner if it's a correct or incorrect sentence (see example).

Extra activity (all classes)

Practice superlative adjectives; review vocabulary

- Write a group of words from a recently studied vocabulary set on the board, e.g.
  guitar   keyboard   bass   drums
- Students take turns to make sentences with superlative adjectives about each word or phrase, e.g. *Drums are the loudest instrument*.

➡ **Workbook page 25**

➡ **Mixed Ability Worksheets page 12**

Building the topic

Vocabulary

> ### Aims
> Present and practice travel activities
> Model *have to / can't* for rules
> Model *don't have to / can* for choices

Cultural note

- **The Great Wall of China** was built from 500 BC until the beginning of the 17th century, in order to protect the country from invaders. Several walls referred to as the Great Wall of China were built. The Great Wall is the world's largest man-made structure and is 6,352 km long. The wall is visible from outer space.

Warm-up

What do students know about the Great Wall of China? How old is it? Why was it built?

1 **Presentation of vocabulary set: travel activities**

- Look at the pictures.
- Read the words and phrases in the box.
- Write the number of the correct picture next to each word or phrase.
- Listen, check and repeat.

🎧 **Answers / Audio CD 1 track 41**

1 drop litter
2 buy a ticket
3 carry your passport
4 camp
5 use a credit card
6 take a tour
7 bargain
8 follow the rules

2 **Comprehension of text (first reading)**

- Read the statements.
- Read and listen to the advice.
- Circle *T* (True) or *F* (False).

🎧 **Audio CD 1 track 42**

Answers

1	F	4	F
2	T	5	T
3	F		

Extend your vocabulary (Workbook page 26)

➡ **Workbook page 26**

Grammar

Aims
Present and practice *have to / can't*
Talk about rules
Present and practice *don't have to / can*
Talk about choices

1 Grammar chart: *have to / can't*

Note:
- We use *have to* to talk about obligations, e.g. *At my school you have to wear a uniform.*
- We use *can't* to talk about things that are not allowed or are forbidden, e.g *At my school you can't wear jeans*.
- We use the infinitive of the verb after *have to* and *can't*.
- See Grammar summary page 115.

2 Controlled practice of *have to / can't*
- Read the sentences.
- Circle the correct verb in each sentence, *have to* or *can't*.

Answers
1 can't	4 can't
2 have to	5 have to
3 Do you have to	

3 Grammar chart: *don't have to / can*

Note:
- We use *don't have to* to talk about things that aren't necessary, e.g *I don't have to do the homework tonight.* (= I have a choice. I can do it tomorrow.)
- We use *can* to talk about things that are possible, e.g. *You can do your homework at the weekend.* (= You are allowed to do it at the weekend.)
- See Grammar summary page 115.

4 Controlled practice of *don't have to / can*
- Look at the pictures.
- Use the icons to fill in the blanks with *can* or *don't have to* and a verb in the box.

Answers
1 don't have to wear	4 don't have to take
2 can have	5 can choose
3 can skate	6 don't have to give

Finished?
Fast finishers can do Puzzle 6B on page 107.

Answers
YOU CAN'T BE SAD. YOU HAVE TO HAVE FUN!

Over to you!

5 Personalization; oral practice of *have to / can't*
- Think of a rule for your school.
- Draw a sign to represent your rule.
- Show your sign to the class.
- The class tries to guess your rule.

Extra activity (all classes)

Practice *have to / don't have to, can / can't*
- Ask students to imagine they are interviewing for a job in the school, e.g. a teacher or even a student.
- Students write sentences about the qualities an applicant needs for the job, e.g. for a teacher:
  You have to be patient and friendly.
  You don't have to wear a suit.
  You can go home at 4 o'clock.
  You can't wear shorts.

➡ **Workbook page 27**

➡ **Mixed Ability Worksheets page 13**

Living English

Reading

 Audio CD 1 track 43

Cultural note

- **Sweden** is a country in northern Europe. Its capital is Stockholm and its population is 9 million. Gothenburg is the second largest city.
- **Scotland** is a country north of England. Its capital is Edinburgh and its population is 5.2 million. Glasgow is the second largest city.
- **Mexico** is a country between North and Central America. Its capital is Mexico City and its population is 108 million.

Warm-up

Books closed. What are students favourite places in their country or abroad? Why do they like them? Are they cool? Why? Would they like to live in these places?

Before you read

1 Pre-reading task

- Look at the photos and the article.
- Answer the question.

Answers

The article is about young people's favorite places around the world.

While you read

2 Presentation and practice of reading skill (first reading)

- Read the reading skills box.

> **Reading skills: Finding specific information**
> Nouns contain the main information in a text. If you learn to look for them in a text, you will find the answers to questions more quickly.

- Read the nouns.
- Read the text quickly.
- In two minutes, write the numbers of the paragraph(s) where you find the nouns next to each one.

Answers

1	students: 2	4	music: 1 and 2
2	sports: 1 and 2	5	museums: 1
3	beaches: 3		

After you read

3 Detailed comprehension task (second reading)

- Read the statements.
- Read the article again.
- Write the name of the town (*Gothenburg*, *Glasgow* and *Cancun*) next to each statement.

Answers

1	Glasgow	4	Cancun
2	Gothenburg	5	Glasgow
3	Cancun	6	Gothenburg

Listening

1 Global comprehension of listening text (first listening)

- Listen to the conversation.
- Answer the question.

🎧 **Audio CD 1 track 44**

Tim:	Hi, Katy. How do you like your new school?
Katy:	Oh, hey Tim. It's really good. I love it there.
Tim:	Really? What's so great about it?
Katy:	Well, the classes are smaller than at the old school. And they have a really good theater group.
Tim:	Cool. I see you have to wear a uniform.
Katy:	Yeah, but it's OK.
Tim:	What about the teachers?
Katy:	They're totally cool. I think they're the best in the city.
Tim:	Is there a lot of homework?
Katy:	We have to do about three hours every night.
Tim:	Whoa! That's a lot.
Katy:	Not really. Anyway, we don't have to take tests. We can do projects instead. I really love that.

Answer

Katy

2 Detailed comprehension of listening text (second listening)

- Read the statements.
- Listen to the conversation again.
- Circle *T* (True) or *F* (False).

🎧 **Audio CD 1 track 44**

Answers

1	T	4	F
2	F	5	F
3	T	6	T

Writing

1 General comprehension of writing model

- Read the brochure quickly.
- Answer the questions.

Answers

Oaxaca in Mexico

Three of the these reasons: It has some of the highest mountains, the most beautiful beaches and the friendliest people. The climate is wonderful, the food is delicious and the shopping is incredible.

2 Detailed comprehension of writing model

- Look at the chart.
- Read the brochure again.
- Fill in the chart with the missing information.

Answers

General	Tips
highest mountains, most beautiful beaches, friendliest people, wonderful climate, delicious food, incredible shopping	Money: American dollars / Mexican pesos, *bargain for cheaper prices* Drink: can't drink tap water, use bottled water Weather: don't have to bring warm clothes, wear sun cream

3 Preparation for personalized writing

- Think about a place you know.
- Copy the chart and fill it in with general information about the place and your tips for visitors.

4 Personalized writing

- Follow the writing model.
- Use your information from the chart in exercise 3.
- Write a brochure about your place.
- Find a photo of the place and add it to your brochure.

➡ **Tests page 12**

6 Review

Vocabulary

1
1 small
2 nice
3 large
4 narrow
5 tall
6 crowded
7 deep
8 long

2
1 bargain (for souvenirs)
2 buy a ticket
3 camp
4 drop litter
5 carry your passport
6 use a credit card
7 follow the rules
8 take a tour

Grammar

1
1 The longest
2 The widest
3 The smallest
4 The most expensive
5 the most crowded
6 the fastest

2
1 You can't take photographs.
2 You have to check large bags.
3 You can't leave young children alone.
4 You can't touch the works of art.
5 You have to arrive at least 30 minutes before closing.
6 You have to buy tickets for special exhibits.

3
1 can
2 don't have to
3 don't have to
4 can

Reading

1
1 The Antarctic.
2 You can go on an Antarctic cruise.
3 You have to go November through March.
4 You can see whales, seals and penguins.
5 You can also visit Argentina.

7 Crime scene

Unit summary

Active vocabulary

- conflict verbs: argue, fight, hide, hit, shout
- places: apartment, bank, fire escape, garage, police station, street corner

Passive vocabulary

- nouns: burglar, bus stop, clown costume, convenience store, dummy, evening news, freeway, gas station, gun, knife, owner, recording, sidewalk, theft, webcam, witness
- verbs: arrest, blow, drop, hold, stand
- adjectives: smart, wrecked
- other: You're kidding, No way

Grammar

- past progressive (affirmative / negative)
- past progressive (questions)

Skills

- Reading witnesses' statements about crimes
- Reading about not-so-sharp criminals
- Reading about someone who lives in a village and in a city
- Listen to two teenagers telling a story
- Talk about activities you were doing at a time in the past
- Using intonation to express surprise

Cross-curricular

- citizenship

Values

- citizenship, ethics,

Exploring the topic

Vocabulary

> **Aims**
> Present and practice conflict verbs
> Recycle irregular plurals of nouns

Warm-up

Books closed. Who was the last person students argued with? Why did they argue? What happened? Summarize new vocabulary on the board.

1 Presentation of vocabulary set: conflict verbs

- Look at the photos.
- Write the correct number next to the verbs.
- Listen, check and repeat.

🎧 **Answers / Audio CD 2 Track 2**

1	shout	4	hit
2	argue	5	hide
3	fight		

Recycling

2 Review plurals of irregular nouns

- Read the nouns.
- Write the plurals.

Answers

1	men	3	children
2	women		

Extra activity (weaker classes)

Further practice of plurals of nouns (regular / irregular)

- Ask students to write a list of ten singular nouns from the book.
- Students swap their list with a partner.
- Students write the plurals of the nouns on their partner's list.
- Students check their answers with their partner.

Extend your vocabulary (Workbook page 28)

> ➡ Workbook page 28

Exploring the topic

Reading

 Audio CD 2 track 3

Warm-up

Have students ever witnessed a crime or an accident?
What happened? What do witnesses usually have to
do? Tell students they are going to read three witness
statements about a crime.

1 Preteach key vocabulary; raise interest

- Read the words.
- Look at the picture and find the things.

Answers
1 on the sidewalk by the woman with the phone
2 held by the man in the bottom right
3 between the woman with the umbrella and the
   woman on the phone
4 both sides of the road
5 the blue car in the road

**2 General comprehension (first reading);
exposure to past progressive (affirmative /
negative)**

- Read and listen to the statements.
- Answer the question.

Answers
Witness C

Extra activity (weaker classes)

Further comprehension

- Write the questions on the board.
- Students read the texts again and write the correct
  witness(es).
  Who:
  1 is the owner of a shop?
  2 was waiting for a bus?
  3 mentions the weather?
  4 saw a gun?
  5 was inside a car?
  6 saw the woman using a cellphone?

Answers
1 Witness C
2 Witness A
3 Witness A
4 Witness A and witness C
5 Witness B
6 Witness A and witness C

Grammar

Aims

Present and practice past progressive
(affirmative / negative)
Talk about actions in progress in the past

1 Grammar chart: past progressive (affirmative / negative)

Note:
- We form the past progressive with subject + *was / wasn't, were / weren't* + *-ing* form of the verb.
- We use the past progressive to talk about actions that are in progress around a specific time. Compare *I argued with my sister yesterday* and *I was arguing with my sister at 6 o'clock.*
- See Grammar summary page 115.

2 Controlled practice of past progressive auxiliary

- Read the paragraph.
- Choose the correct form of *be*.

Answers

1	wasn't	4	were
2	was	5	was
3	were	6	weren't

3 Controlled practice of past progressive (affirmative / negative)

- Look at the picture.
- Read the sentences.
- Fill in the blanks with the past progressive of the verbs in parentheses.

Answers
1 wasn't dancing
2 were playing a video game
3 weren't singing
4 was eating
5 wasn't working on the computer
6 wasn't crying

4 Controlled practice of past progressive (affirmative / negative)

- Read the dialog.
- Fill in the gaps with the past progressive of the verbs in brackets.

Answers

1	was talking	5	were sending
2	wasn't talking	6	wasn't sending
3	was reading	7	wasn't watching
4	weren't reading		

Finished?

Fast finishers can do Puzzle 7A on page 109.

Answers
From left to right: Lucy, Yomi, Ryan, Adam

Over to you!

5 Personalization; written and oral practice of *past progressive (affirmative / negative)*

- Write two true sentences and one false sentence using about yesterday using the past progressive affirmative and negative.
- Take turns to tell the class (see example).
- Are the students' statements true or false?

Extra activity (all classes)

Past progressive practice

- Find a picture or pictures with lots of activities, e.g. page 22.
- Ask students to look at the picture for one minute.
- Ask students questions about the picture, e.g. *What was Nancy wearing?*
- Which student would make the best witness?

Note:
- Stronger classes can write down everything that was happening in the picture/s that they can remember.

➡ Workbook page 29

➡ Mixed Ability Worksheets page 14

Building the topic

Vocabulary

Warm-up

Tell students the police have caught the suspects for
the crime they read about on page 58. Ask students to
look at the pictures of the suspects. Which do they
think is guilty of a crime? Why?

1 Presentation of vocabulary set: places

- Look at the pictures.
- Fill in the blanks with the places in the box.
- Listen, check and repeat.

🎧 **Answers / Audio CD 2 track 4**

1	bank	4	garage
2	apartment	5	street corner
3	fire escape	6	police station

2 Vocabulary practice; exposure to past progressive (questions)

- Read the interviews.
- Look at the pictures and answer the question.

🎧 **Audio CD 2 track 5**

Answers
Ellen and Jason are telling the truth.

3 Comprehension of text (second reading)

- Read the statements.
- Choose *T* (True) or *F* (False) for each statement.

Answers

1	T	4	F
2	F	5	T
3	F		

Extend your vocabulary (Workbook page 30)

➡ **Workbook page 30**

Grammar

Aims
Present and practice past progressive (*Yes / No* questions and short answers, *wh-*questions)
Asking about actions in progress in the past

1 Grammar chart: past progressive (questions)

Note:
- We form *yes / no* questions in the past progressive by swapping the verb *be* and the subject, e.g. *He was studying.* ➡ *Was he studying?*
- We make short answers with *Yes / No* + subject pronoun + *was / wasn't, were / weren't*. We do not use another verb in short answers, e.g. *Were you listening? Yes, I was / No, I wasn't.* NOT ~~Yes, I was listening.~~ or ~~No, I wasn't listening.~~
- We form *wh-* questions in the past progressive by adding a *wh-* word to the beginning of a *yes / no* question.
- See Grammar summary page 115.

2 Controlled practice of past progressive questions

- Read the skeleton questions.
- Write questions in the past progressive.

Answers
1 What were you doing at seven p.m.?
2 Was he talking to Marcy last night?
3 What were they watching on TV yesterday afternoon?
4 Where was she going yesterday morning?
5 Why were they running?
6 Was he arguing with Fran last week?

3 Further practice of past progressive

- Read the answers.
- Write the number of the corresponding question in exercise 2 next to each answer.

Answers
1	3	4	5
2	2	5	6
3	1	6	4

4 Further controlled practice of past progressive (*wh-* questions)

- Read the answers and look at the underlined part.
- Write *wh-* questions for the answers.

Answers
1 What were you looking for?
2 Why was Tyler running?
3 Where were they waiting for us?
4 What was he watching?
5 Where were you going?
6 What were do you doing at twelve o'clock yesterday?

Finished?

Fast finishers can do Puzzle 7B on page 109.

Answers
1 bank
2 apartment
3 garage
4 fire escape

police station

Over to you!

5 Personalization; oral practice of past progressive (*wh-* questions)

- Look at the phrases in the box.
- Take turns to ask your partner questions and respond appropriately (see example).

Answers
Students' own answers

Extra activity (stronger classes)

Practice of past progressive (affirmative / negative and questions)

- This is a variation of the extra activity on page 59.
- Students work in pairs.
- One student looks at the picture and tries to memorize as much as possible.
- The other student prepares questions in the past progressive about the picture.
- Students take turns to ask questions and answer about a picture.

➡ **Workbook page 31**

➡ **Mixed Ability Worksheets page 15**

Living English

Reading

 Audio CD 2 track 6

Cultural note
- **Colorado** see page 36, Building the topic.

Warm-up
What famous crimes do students know about? Have they heard of any famous criminals and what they did?

Before you read

1 Pre-reading task

- Look at the pictures.
- Read the title and the introduction.
- Answer the question.

Answers
b

While you read

2 Comprehension task (first reading)

- Read the summaries of the stories.
- Write the number of the story next to each summary.

Answers

1	4	3	2
2	1	4	3

After you read

3 Detailed comprehension task (second reading)

- Read the statements.
- Read the stories again and choose *T* (True) or *F* (False).

Answers

1	T	3	F
2	F	4	T

Extra activity (stronger classes)

Further comprehension of text

- Write the questions on the board.
  1. How did the man know a burglar was stealing his computer?
  2. Why did the police stop the driver on the freeway?
  3. What was his punishment?
  4. Why did the thieves return to the gas station?
  5. How did the police find the convenience store robbers?
- Students answer the questions.

Answers
1. His webcam was recording the burglar.
2. Because the passenger wasn't moving or talking.
3. The police fined him $115.
4. Because they were low on gas.
5. One of the robbers entered a contest with her real name, address and phone number.

Listening

1 Presentation of listening skill (first listening)

- Read the Listening skills box.
- Look at the pictures.
- Identify as many words as possible that you might hear in the conversation.
- Read the list of words.
- Listen to the conversation.
- Write *G* (Gwen) or *M* (Maria) next to each word.

Listening skills: Predicting vocabulary

- Predicting key words that you might hear in a listening helps you to prepare to understand the important events in a listening.

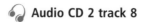 **Audio CD 2 track 7**

Maria:	What were *you* doing at midnight last night, Gwen?
Gwen:	I was sleeping. Then the whole room was shaking, and things were falling off the shelves. I was shouting "Help!" because I was really scared. What were you doing last night, Maria?
Maria:	I was driving home from work.
Gwen:	What happened?
Maria:	Suddenly the car was going up and down. I thought something was wrong with the car! But then people were running out of their houses and I realized it was an earthquake.

Answers

1	G	4	M
2	G	5	G / M
3	M		

2 Comprehension of listening text (second listening)

- Read the sentences.
- Listen again and choose the correct words.

Answers

1	sleeping	4	driving
2	shouting	5	people running
3	scared		

Speaking

1 First listening

- Look at the pictures and read the model dialogs.
- Listen and read.

Audio CD 2 track 8

2 Presentation of pronunciation point

> **Pronunciation: Expressing surprise**
> - When you are surprised, the intonation in sentences changes more than in normal sentences. Conversely, when you are not at all surprised, the intonation changes less, i.e. the sentence is "flatter" than normal.

- Read the example sentences.
- Listen and repeat, copying the intonation.

Audio CD 2 track 9

3 Pronunciation practice

- Read the sentences.
- Listen and write ✓ next to sentences that express surprise and write ✗ next to sentences that don't express surprise.

Answers / Audio CD 2 track 10

1	That's boring. ✗	4	That's interesting. ✗
2	You're kidding. ✓	5	No way! ✓
3	That's amazing. ✓		

4 Dialog practice

- Practice the model dialogs with another student.
- Change roles and practice again.

5 Dialog personalization and practice

- Look at the words in blue in the model dialog.
- Think of some different activities.
- Replace the blue words with your ideas to make a new dialog.
- Practice the dialog with another student, expressing surprise where appropriate.

➡ **Tests page 14**

7

Review

Vocabulary

1
1 argue
2 hit
3 hiding
4 shout
5 fighting

2
1 F
2 D
3 E
4 C
5 A
6 B

Grammar

1
1 They weren't running.
2 Josh was looking at a map.
3 Mariel was driving.
4 Josh was talking on the phone.
5 Mariel was shouting.
6 They weren't laughing.

2
1 What were you doing
2 Where were you going
3 Why were you going there
4 Was Josh riding with you?
5 Were you arguing?
6 Why were you arguing?

Study skills

1
Spelling 1
Stress 2
Pronunciation 3
Part of speech 4
Definition / meaning 5
Example 6

Survivors

Unit summary

Active vocabulary

- Natural disasters: blizzard, earthquake, flood, forest fire, hailstorm, hurricane, tornado, tsunami
- Adverbs of manner: angrily, carefully, happily, hard, ice, loudly, quickly, quietly, well
- nouns: hunter, rope, serve, survivor, wing
- verbs: catch fire, go to hospital, make an emergency call, private, serve

Passive vocabulary

- nouns: bravery, connection, controls, couple, determination, distance, downstairs, effect, flight attendant, girlfriend, ice cap, lawn mower, rope, view
- verbs: annoy, come out, destroy, go up, hang, melt, predict, survive, take action,
- adjective: confused, extreme, normal, polar
- advert: alone, patiently

Grammar

- past progressive and simple past
- adverbs of manner

Skills

- Reading about an action movie
- Reading about a crime
- Read about survivors of a climbing accident
- Listen to the story of a plane accident
- Using sequence words: *first, then, next* and *finally*
- Write about a favorite movie

Cross-curricular

- geography, science

Values

- environmental awareness

Introducing the topic

Vocabulary

> ### Aims
> Present and practice natural disasters vocabulary

Warm-up

How many natural disasters can students think of? Do they know anything about the places they commonly occur in? Have students ever witnessed a natural disaster? What happened?

1 Presentation of vocabulary set: natural disasters

- Look at the photos.
- Write the correct number next to each disaster.
- Listen, check and repeat.

Answers / Audio CD 2 track 11

1	earthquake	5	blizzard
2	tsumani	6	hailstorm
3	tornado	7	flood
4	forest fire	8	hurricane

Recycling

2 Review of natural disasters vocabulary

- Look at the chart.
- Write the words from exercise 1 in the correct column.

Answers

fire	wind	water	earth
forest fire	tornado	blizzard	earthquake
	hurricane	flood	
	blizzard	tsunami	
		hailstorm	

Extend your vocabulary (Workbook page 32)

➡ **Workbook page 32**

Exploring the topic

Aims
Present and review past progressive and simple past
Review natural disasters vocabulary

Reading

 Audio CD 2 track 12

Cultural note

- **The Day After Tomorrow** is a science fiction movie released in 2004. It shows the disastrous effects of global cooling (the earth getting colder). It starred Dennis Quaid and Jake Gyllenhaal and earned over $500 million.

Warm-up

Do students know what a "disaster movie" is? What disaster movies have students seen? What was the disaster in them? What happened?

1 **Comprehension (first reading); exposure to past progressive and simple past**

- Read the sentences.
- Read the text and put a number 1–5 next to each sentence.

Answers
Scientists and world leaders were discussing the weather changes. 1
Scientist Jack predicted a new Ice Age. 2
Natural disasters were happening all over the world. 3
Jack started a long journey to save his son. 4
The sun came out and the weather changed again. 5

2 **Detailed comprehension (second reading)**

- Read the sentences.
- Read the text again.
- Fill in the blanks with the words in the box.

Answers
1 A tsunami   4 Hailstorms
2 Hurricanes   5 Tornadoes
3 Blizzards

Grammar

Aims
Present, contrast and practice past progressive and past simple (affirmative and negative)
Talk about actions in progress and completed actions

1 Grammar chart: past progressive and simple past

Note:
- We use the past progressive to describe longer actions that occur around a specific point in time.
- We use the simple past for actions that started and finished in the past.
- In the negative, the past progressive takes the negative form of *be*.
- The negative of the simple past is made with *did not*.
- Actions in the past progressive are often interrupted by an event in the simple past, e.g. *I was having dinner when the doorbell rang.*
- See Grammar summary page 115.

2 Exposure to actions in progress and completed actions
- Read the sentences.
- Match the actions in progress 1–6 with the completed actions A–F.

Answers

1	C	3	F
2	E	4	A
3	B	6	D

3 Controlled practice of past progressive for actions in progress
- Read the first part of the story.
- Fill in the blanks with the present progressive of the verbs in parentheses.

Answers

1	were flying	4	were serving
2	was working	5	were watching
3	were checking	6	were reading

4 Controlled practice of simple past for completion actions
- Read the second part of the story.

- Fill in the blanks with the simple past of the verbs in parentheses.

Answers

1	started	4	called
2	went	5	didn't answer
3	looked	6	hit

Finished?
Fast finishers can do Puzzle 8A on page 109.

Answers

FLOO**D**	HAIL**S**TORM
HURR**I**CANE	EAR**T**HQUAKE
T**S**UNAMI	FOR**E**STFIRE
BLIZZ**A**RD	TO**R**NADO

Mystery word: DISASTER

Over to you!

5 Personalization; oral practice of past progressive and past simple
- Think about a good and bad dream.
- Take turns to tell your partner about it (see example) using the past progressive for actions in progress and the past simple for completed actions.

Extra activity (stronger classes)

Practice past progressive and simple past
- Think of a crime, where and when it happened. Tell the students about the crime and describe two "suspects" that were seen near the crime scene. Make sure the description corresponds to the two stronger students in the class. The two "suspects" will be questioned by the remainder of the class: the "detectives".
- The two suspects leave the classroom and decide where they were at the time of the crime and what they were doing together.
- The detectives prepare questions for the suspects.
- After five minutes, bring the first suspect into the class.
- The detectives question the suspect and take notes.
- Then bring the next suspect into the class.
- The detectives question the second suspect.
- If the suspects' stories are the same, they are innocent. If the suspects' stories are different or contradict each other, they are guilty.

➡ **Workbook page 33**

➡ **Mixed Ability Worksheets page 16**

Building the topic

Vocabulary

> ### Aims
> Present and practice adverbs of manner
> Model the position of adverbs of manner

Warm-up

Ask students to read the first two paragraphs of the story. Have they ever been in a similar situation? What did they do? or What would they do?

1 Presentation of vocabulary set: adverbs of manner.

- Look at the pictures.
- Write the correct number of the picture next to each adverb.
- Listen, check and repeat.

🎧 **Answers / Audio CD 2 track 13**

1	happily	5	quickly / hard
2	angrily	6	carefully
3	quietly	7	well
4	loudly		

2 Comprehension of reading text

- Read the statements.
- Read and listen to the text.
- Choose *T* (True) or *F* (False) for each sentence.

🎧 **Audio CD 2 track 14**

Answers		
1 F	4 F	
2 F	5 T	
3 T		

Extra activity (stronger classes)

Revision of vocabulary

- Think of five different categories of vocabulary that students have studied recently, e.g. adverbs, disasters, places, etc.
- In pairs, students write a list of the categories.
- Tell students they are going to write a list of words in the categories beginning with a specific letter.
- Tell students a letter, e.g. *F*
- Students write down a word in each of the categories, e.g. *funnily* (adverbs), *forest fire* (disasters), *fire escape* (places), etc.

- Stop students after a suitable time limit, e.g. 30 seconds.
- Feedback on the board with the words for each category.
- Each pair scores a point for each unique word they wrote down and zero points for any words that other students wrote too.
- Give students another letter and restart the activity.

Extend your vocabulary (Workbook page 34)

> ➡ **Workbook page 34**

Grammar

Aims
Present and practice *adverbs of manner*
Talk about how we do things

1 Grammar chart: adverbs of manner

Note:
- Adverbs of manner describe they way we do something, e.g. *I speak English well.*
- Regular adverbs are made by the adjective + *ly*, e.g. *bad ➡ badly.*
- Adjectives that end in –*y*, we replace the *y* with *i* and add –*ly*, e.g. *happy ➡ happily.*
- Some adverbs are irregular, e.g. *good ➡ well, hard ➡ hard, fast ➡ fast.*
- See Grammar summary page 116.

2 Exposure to the relationship between adjectives and adverbs; controlled practice of adverbs

- Read the sentences.
- Fill in the blanks with the adverbs of the adjectives in the first sentence.

Answers

1	carefully	3	well	5	angrily
2	happily	4	fast	6	hard

3 Controlled practice of adverbs

- Read the adjectives in the box.
- Look at the pictures.
- Fill in the blanks with the adverb forms of the adjectives in the box.

Answers

1	hard	3	fast	5	well
2	badly	4	loudly	6	angrily

Take note!

Adjective and adverbs

- Adjectives describe nouns and usually take the following positions:
  - before a noun, e.g. *It was a scary hurricane.*
  - after the verb *be*, e.g. *That hurricane was scary.*
- Adverbs of manner describe the way we do things. They come at end of the verb phrases, e.g. *The tsunami hit the coast quickly.*

Extra activity (all classes)

Practice of adverbs of manner

- Students work in groups of three.
- Student A writes an adverb of manner on a piece of paper and gives it to student B e.g. *Slowly.*
- Student C gives student B a command, e.g. *Stand up!*
- Student B performs the action in the manner described by the adverb, e.g. he / she stands up slowly.
- Student C tries to guess the adverb.
- Students swap roles and begin the activity again.

4 Further practice of adjectives and adverbs

- Read the paragraph.
- Choose the correct words.

Answers

1	slowly	5	brave
2	beautiful	6	slowly
3	happy	7	good
4	kindly	8	patiently

Finished?

Fast finishers can do Puzzle 8B on page 109.

Answers
Toby plays the guitar loudly.

Over to you!

5 Personalization; oral practice of *adverbs*

- Say something you did in the past.
- Take turns to guess the appropriate adverbs (see example).

➡ **Workbook page 35**

➡ **Mixed Ability Worksheets page 17**

Living English

Aims

Read about surviving a storm
Practice organising writing into paragraphs
Use a chart to plan your writing
Talk about things you like and what you are doing right now
Use appropriate sentence stress

Reading

 Audio CD 2 track 15

Cultural note

- **Touching the Void** is a book by Joe Simpson about his near fatal attempt to climb the Siula Grande mountain in 1985. It was published in 1988. Fifteen years later a documentary film was made.
- **Siula Grande** is a mountain in the Peruvian Andes. It is 6,344 meters high.
- **Peru** is a country in western South America. Its capital is Lima and its population is 28 million.

Warm-up

Have students ever been climbing? Where did they go? How high did they climb? Did anything happen? Explain the situation in *Touching the Void* to the students and ask them what they would do in the same situation. Would they cut the rope?

Before you read

1 Pre-reading task

- Read the words and check their meaning.
- Put the things in order of importance (1= the most important).
- Discuss the answers in class.

Answers
Students' own answers

While you read

2 General comprehension (first reading)

- Read the events.
- Read and listen to the story.
- Put the correct number of the event next to each sentence.

Answers
Yates and Simpson climbed Siula Grande. 1
Simpson fell and broke his leg. 2
Yates and Simpson went down tied together with a rope. 3
A snowstorm hit the mountain. 4
Both climbers survived. 5

After you read

3 Detailed comprehension (second reading)

- Read the newspaper report.
- Read the story again.
- Fill in the blanks with the words in the box.

Answers

1	Siula Grande	5	cut
2	leg	6	ice
3	rope	7	survived
4	snowstorm	8	book

Listening

Cultural note

- **David Coulthard** (born March 27, 1971) is a British Formula One racing driver from Scotland. He has driven for Williams, McLaren and Red Bull racing teams.
- **Tom Cruise** (born July 3, 1962) is a very successful movie actor. His most famous films include: *Top Gun, The Mission: Impossible films* and *War of the Worlds.*
- **The War of the Worlds** is a science fiction story written by the British author H. G. Wells in 1898. In 1938, a radio adaptation of the story on American radio caused a panic when people thought that aliens had actually landed on earth.

1 Raise interest in listening text

- Look at the photos.
- Answer the questions.

Audio CD 2 track 16

British racing driver David Coulthard was flying over France in his private jet. He was traveling with his girlfriend. They were going on vacation. Then the pilot made an emergency call. The plane had a problem. They had to land immediately. Then things got worse, and the plane caught fire. David helped his girlfriend escape the fire. They both escaped quickly through a window. A rescue team took them to hospital.

Answers

A formula one racing driver

2 Comprehension of listening text (first listening)

- Read the sentences.
- Listen again and choose the correct answer.

Answers

A

3 Detailed comprehension of listening text (second listening)

- Read the sentences and the words in the box.
- Listen again.
- Fill in the blanks with the words in the box.

Answers

1	France	4	made an emergency call
2	private jet	5	caught fire
3	his girlfriend	6	went to hospital

Writing

1 Presentation of writing skill

- Read the Writing skills box.

> **Writing skills: *first*, *then*, *next* and *finally***
> - Using sequencing words such as *first, then, next* and *finally* helps to organize your writing. These words also signal to the reader the stages of a story.

2 General comprehension of writing model

- Read the jumbled writing model.
- Put the correct number next to each paragraph.

Answers

1	Ray Ferrier ...	3	Next, Ray decided ...
2	First, a big storm ...	4	Finally, Ray caused ...

3 Detailed comprehension of writing model

- Read the text again.
- Fill in the chart with information about *War of the Worlds.*

Answers

War of the Worlds

Characters and place:	Ray – Father (Tom Cruise)
	Rachel – Daughter
	Robbie – Son
Place:	Boston
What happened:	First, a big storm hit Ray's neighbourhood.
Next:	Ray decided to take his children back to Boston.
Then:	A group of aliens caught Ray and Rachel.
The End:	Finally, Ray caused an explosion and destroyed the aliens

4 Preparation for personalized writing

- Copy the chart in exercise 3.
- Fill in the chart with information about a movie you like.

5 Personalized writing

- Follow the writing model and use the chart in exercise 4 to write about a movie you like.
- Use *first, then, next* and *finally* to sequence events.

➡ Tests page 16

8 Review

Vocabulary

1
1. tornado
2. blizzard
3. hurricane
4. forest fire
5. tsunami
6. flood
7. earthquake
8. hailstorm

2
1. fast
2. angrily
3. quietly
4. well
5. hard

Grammar

1
1. was walking
2. was shining
3. were singing
4. were playing
5. were playing
6. was listening

2
1. hit
2. started
3. flew
4. ran
5. drove
6. went
7. had
8. waited

3
1. loudly
2. happily
3. carefully
4. easily
5. well
6. hard

Reading

1
1. T
2. F
3. F
4. F
5. T
6. T

9 The sporting life

Unit summary

Active vocabulary

- Exercise verbs: bend, hit, jump, kick, land, pass, spin, stretch, warm up
- Sports: do track, do karate, go cycling, go horseback riding, go water-skiing, play basketball, play golf, play lacrosse
- nouns: fence, gymnastics, kung fu

Passive vocabulary

- nouns: goals, martial art, moves, muscles, net, opponent, rattan, trick
- adjectives: complicated
- verbs: need, prevent, quit

Grammar

- *should / shouldn't*
- *going to*

Skills

- Reading about an unusual sport
- Reading about some teenagers' summer sports resolutions
- Reading about a teenager and kung fu
- Learn about references to the subject using pronouns
- Listen to an interview about travel adventures
- Talk about summer plans
- Pronounce words with silent letters correctly

Cross-curricular

- sport, science,

Values

- looking after your physical well-being

Introducing the topic
Vocabulary

> **Aims**
> Present and practice exercise verbs
> Review parts of the body vocabulary

Warm-up

Books closed. Ask students to imagine they are going to play / do their favourite sport. Students write three things they do *before* they start the sport. Do students warm up before playing sport? Why? What happens if you don't warm up?

1 Presentation of vocabulary set: exercise verbs

- Look at the pictures.
- Label the pictures with the words in the box.
- Listen, check and repeat.

🎧 **Answers / Audio CD 2 track 17**

1	kick	5	hit
2	pass	6	bend
3	stretch	7	spin
4	jump	8	land

Recycling

2 Review of parts of the body

- Label the parts of the body with the correct words.

Answers

1	hand	4	back
2	arm	5	head
3	leg	6	foot

Extend your vocabulary (Workbook page 36)

> ➡ Workbook page 36

Exploring the topic

Reading

 Audio CD 2 track 18

Culture note

• **Indonesia** – see page 34, Exploring the topic

Warm-up

What do students think the following sports are: *roller football* (football on roller blades), *chessboxing* (six games of chess followed by five rounds of boxing!), *underwater hockey* (hockey played in a swimming pool, with masks and snorkels). Do students know any other unusual sports? Have they ever played any of them?

1 General comprehension (first reading)

• Read the text quickly.
• Answer the question.

Answers
gymnastics, soccer and volleyball

2 Detailed comprehension (second reading)

• Read the sentences.
• Read and listen to the text.
• Fill in the blanks with correct words from the text.

Answers

1	Indonesia	4	warm up / stretch
2	three	5	gymnastics
3	shorts	6	heads

Extra activity (stronger classes)

Further comprehension

• Write the questions on the board.
  1 What do you need to play sepak takraw?
  2 Why shouldn't you wear long shorts?
  3 Why should you warm up before playing?
  4 How do you win points?
• Students answer the questions.

Answers
1 You need a ball, a volleyball net and six players.
2 Because you have to kick high and move your legs a lot.
3 Because if your muscles are warm before you play, you can prevent injuries.
4 When you hit the ball onto the floor of your opponents' side of the net.

Grammar

Aims

Present and practice *should / shouldn't*
(affirmative, negative and questions)
Give advice

1 Grammar chart: *should / shouldn't*

Note:
- We use *should / shouldn't* to give advice.
- *Should* is a modal verb and it is:
  - the same for all subjects, e.g. *He should.* NOT ~~He shoulds.~~
  - followed by a verb in the infinitive without *to*, e.g. *He should go.* NOT ~~He should to go.~~
- The negative is formed with *not,* e.g. *He should not go.*
- *Should + not* is contracted to *shouldn't.*
- Questions are formed by swapping the subject and *should,* e.g. *He should go.* ➡ *Should he go?*
- We do not use *do* or *be* with *should,* e.g. *Should I come?* NOT ~~Do I should come?~~ *I shouldn't tell you.* NOT ~~I don't should tell you.~~

See Grammar summary page 116.

2 Controlled practice of *should / shouldn't* (affirmative / negative)

- Read the advice and look at the pictures.
- Choose the correct word in each sentence: *should* or *shouldn't.*

Answers

1	should	4	should
2	shouldn't	5	should
3	should	6	should

3 Controlled practice of *should / shouldn't* (affirmative / negative)

- Read the sentences.
- Put the words in order to make advice about studying.

Answers
1 You should sit at a desk.
2 You should take regular breaks.
3 You shouldn't study for a long time.
4 You should use a good light.
5 You shouldn't watch TV.
6 You shouldn't lie down.

4 Controlled practice of *should / shouldn't* (questions)

- Read the dialogs.
- Look at the skeleton phrases in parentheses.
- Complete the questions.

Answers
1 When should I go
2 What should I do
3 Should I take lessons
4 Should we study together
5 Where should I go

Finished?

Fast finishers can do Puzzle 9A on page 109

Answers

jump, kick, land, pass, spin, stretch, bend

Missing verb = hit

Over to you!

5 Personalization; written practice of *should / shouldn't*

- Work in groups.
- Each person writes three sentences giving advice about how to be good at sports.
- Compare the sentences and choose the best.
- Make a poster of your group's advice.

Extra activity (all classes)

Free practice of *should / shouldn't*

- Ask students to imagine they are giving advice to a new student or teacher starting at their school.
- In groups, students write sentences giving advice using *should / shouldn't,* e.g. *You shouldn't forget your sports kit.*
- Compare the sentences in the class. Which group has the best advice?

➡ **Workbook page 37**

➡ **Mixed Ability Worksheets page 18**

Building the topic

Vocabulary

Aims

Present and practice sports
Model *going to* for plans and resolutions
Read a text about teenagers' summer sports resolutions

Cultural note

- **Lacrosse** is a team sport invented by native North Americans. Each player has a stick with a net and must use it to pass and shoot with a ball. Lacrosse is the fastest growing sport in the United States.

Warm-up

Books closed. Do students make new year's resolutions? Have they ever made resolutions about anything else? Ask students to make a sports resolution for next year. What are they going to do? Why are they going to do it? Who are they going to do it with?

1 Presentation of vocabulary set: sports

- Look at the photos.
- Read the words in the box.
- Write the correct number of the photos next to the words.
- Listen, check and repeat.

 Answers / Audio CD 2 track 19

1	go cycling	5	do track
2	do karate	6	play basketball
3	play golf	7	go water-skiing
4	go horseback riding	8	play lacrosse

2 Further vocabulary practice

- Read the statements.
- Read and listen to the text.
- Write the name of the person next to each statement.

 Audio CD 2 track 20

Answers

1 Benny
2 Kathy and Josh
3 Geraldo
4 Kyle and Tyler
5 Amelia
6 Kamala
7 Kelly

Extend your vocabulary (Workbook page 38)

➡ **Workbook page 38**

Grammar

Aims

Present and practice *going to*
Talk about plans and resolutions

1 Grammar chart: *going to*

Note:
- We use *going to* talk about plans and resolutions in the future.
- We form sentences with *going to* with subject + *be* + *going to* + infinitive (without *to*).
- We form the negative of *going to* with subject + *be* + *not* + *going to* + infinitive (without *to*).
- We make *yes / no* questions by swapping the subject and *be*, e.g. *He's going to do more exercise?* ➡ *Is he going to do more exercise?*
- We make short answers with *Yes / No* + subject pronoun + *am / 'm not, is / isn't, are / aren't*. We do not contract the subject and *be* in affirmative short answers. e.g. *Are you going to warm up? Yes, I am.* NOT ~~*Yes, I'm.*~~
- We make *wh-* questions by adding a *wh-* word to the beginning of a *yes / no* questions. e.g. *When is he going to do more exercise?*

See Grammar summary page 116.

2 Controlled practice of *going to*.

- Read the sentences.
- Choose the correct form for the blanks in the sentences.

Answers

1 b	2 b	3 a	4 c	5 c

3 Further practice of *going to*

- Read the *Activity Camp* list.
- Complete the sentences with the correct form of *going to*.

Answers

1	She's going to	4	She isn't going to
2	She isn't going to	5	She isn't going to
3	She's going to	6	She's going to

4 Practice of *going to* (*yes / no* questions and *wh-* questions)

- Read the dialog.
- Read the skeleton questions.
- Complete the missing questions in the dialog.

Answers
1 What are you going to do
2 Why are you going to visit
3 How long are you going to stay?
4 Are you going to visit London?
5 Are your grandparents going to come

Finished?

Fast finishers can do Puzzle 9B on page 109.

Answers
TENNIS
VOLLEY BALL

Over to you!

5 Personalization; written and oral practice of *going to*

- Write sentences using *going to* (affirmative and negative) about your plans for next weekend.
- Take turns to ask your partner questions about the weekend and respond appropriately (see example).

Extra activity (stronger classes)

Oral free practice *going to* for future plans

- Write the diary on the board.

	Saturday	Sunday
9-10		
10-11		
11-12		
12-1		
1-2		
2-3		
4-5		
5-6	*go to the movies*	
6-7		

- Ask students to copy and complete the diary with activities they are going to do at the weekend e.g. *go to the movies*, but to leave four spaces blank. Tell students not to show their diaries to their partner.
- In pairs, students ask and answer questions about what they are doing at the weekend until they find a time when they can meet.

➡ **Workbook page 39**

➡ **Mixed Ability Worksheets page 19**

Living English

Aims

Read about a teenager and kung fu
Learn about references to the subject using pronouns
Listen to an interview about travel adventures
Talk about summer plans
Pronounce words with silent letters correctly

Reading

 Audio CD 2 track 21

Cultural note

- **Kung fu** is a term used to describe Chinese martial arts. It means "achievement through great effort".

Warm-up

Books closed. Is any student in the class very dedicated to a particular sport? Which sport? How often do they practice / play? What are their plans for the future?

Before you read

1 Pre-reading task

- Look at the pictures and the title.
- Answer the question.

Answer

kung fu

While you read

2 Present reading skill

Read the reading skills box.

> **Reading skills: Subject reference**
> - Using subject pronouns avoids repeating the noun in your writing and makes your writing more natural.

3 Practice of reading skill

- Find the pronouns in the lines in the text.
- Choose the word that they refer to.

Answers

1	a	4	b
2	b	5	a
3	a		

After you read

4 Detailed comprehension

- Read the sentences.
- Read the article.
- Fill in the blanks with the correct words from the text.

Answers

1	300	4	parents
2	money	5	two
3	junk food	6	martial arts camp

Listening

1 General comprehension (first listening)

- Look at the pictures.
- Listen to the interview.
- Answer the questions.

🎧 Audio CD 2 track 22

Interviewer:	Jason Werner is an adventurous person. He's here today to talk about his next adventure! Welcome, Jason.
Jason:	Thanks.
interviewer:	So, last year you cycled across the United States. What's your next adventure?
Jason:	I'm going to sail a small boat across the Atlantic Ocean.
Interviewer:	Are you going to do that alone?
Jason:	Yes, I am.
Interviewer:	How long is that going to take?
Jason:	It depends on the weather, really. Probably about four months.
Interviewer:	Jason, tell me. What should you do to get ready for this kind of adventure?
Jason:	You should do a lot of exercise. You need to be really strong. And, you should get a lot of information about other people's experiences before you go.
Interviewer:	Well, good luck with your next adventure.

Answers

Last year he cycled across the United States. Next he is going to sail a small boat across the Atlantic Ocean.

2 Detailed comprehension of listening text (second listening)

- Read the sentences.
- Listen again and circle the correct words.

Answers

1	bicycle	3	four months	5	a lot of
2	Atlantic	4	exercise		

Speaking

1 First listening

- Look at the pictures and read the model dialogs.
- Listen and read.

🎧 Audio CD 2 track 23

2 Presentation of pronunciation point

> **Pronunciation: Silent letters**
> - When you say a word, silent letters are letters that you can't hear. There are no rules about silent letters.

- Read the example words.
- Listen and repeat, without pronouncing the silent letters.

🎧 Audio CD 2 track 24

3 Pronunciation practice

- Read the words in the box.
- Listen and cross out the silent letters.
- Listen and repeat.

🎧 Answers / Audio CD 2 Track 25

1	shou~~l~~dn't	4	wa~~l~~k
2	ans~~w~~er	5	ta~~l~~k
3	i~~s~~land		

Extra activity (all classes)

Further practice of silent letters

- Write the following list of words on the board: *honest, design, folk, wrong, listen, knives, autumn, often, climb, calm.*
- In pairs, ask students to practice saying the words. Help students with pronunciation as necessary.
- Students cross out the silent letters in the words.

Answers

~~h~~onest, desi~~g~~n, fol~~k~~, ~~w~~rong, lis~~t~~en, ~~k~~nives, autum~~n~~, of~~t~~en, clim~~b~~, ca~~l~~m

4 Dialog practice

- Practice the model dialogs with another student.
- Change roles and practice again.

5 Dialog personalization and practice

- Look at the words in blue in the model dialog.
- Think of some different summer plans and some advice.
- Replace the blue words with your ideas to make a new dialog.
- Practice the dialog with another student.

➡ Tests page 18

Vocabulary

1
1 bend
2 pass
3 jump
4 kick
5 land
6 stretch
7 spin
8 hit

2
go – water-skiing, horseback riding, cycling
play – basketball, golf, lacrosse
do – karate, track

Grammar

1
1 You should listen to your coach
2 Should I warm up before exercise?
3 She shouldn't eat a lot of fast food.
4 They should wear a helmet.
5 What should I wear to your party?
6 He shouldn't fight with his teammates.

2
1 He is going to practice a lot.
2 He isn't going to stay up late.
3 He is going to eat healthy food.
4 He isn't going to eat a lot of fast food.
5 He is going to listen to the coach.
6 He isn't going to argue with referee

3
1 Are they going to go to the zoo tomorrow?
2 Are you going to do karate this year?
3 Is he going to play soccer this evening?
4 When are we going to go horseback riding?
5 Where are they going to go on vacation this summer?

Study skills

1
2 Student's own answers.

10 The future

Unit summary

Active vocabulary

- Actions: bounce, bump into, catch, climb, dive, drop, float, throw
- Describing planets: close, cold, dangerous, dry, far, safe, stable, unstable, warm, wet

Passive vocabulary

- nouns: ceiling, floor, flying board, gravity, gymnast, orbit, oxygen, polar bear, protection, radiation, soda, stadium, surface, tourism, UV rays
- verbs: evaporate, freeze, fry

Grammar

- *will / won't*
- *too / not enough*

Skills

- Reading about space tourism
- Reading about life on Mars
- Reading about the future of the Earth
- Write about your life in the future
- Talk about your life in the future
- Pronounce *I* /aɪ/ and *I'll* /aɪl/ correctly

Cross-curricular

- geography, science

Values

- environmental awareness

Introducing the topic

Vocabulary

> **Aims**
> Present and practice action verbs

Warm-up

Books closed. Drop something on the floor. Ask why it fell to elicit *gravity*. Ask students to explain what it is. Ask them to imagine there was no gravity. What would happen? Write new vocabulary on the board.

1 **Presentation of vocabulary set: actions**

- Look at the pictures.
- Write the words in the box next to the correct pictures.
- Listen, check and repeat.

Answers / Audio CD 2 track 26

1	throw	5	bump into
2	catch	6	dive
3	bounce	7	float
4	drop	8	climb

Recycling

2 **Practice and review of actions**

- Read the categories.
- Match seven words from exercise 1 with the categories.

Answers

Mountain: climb
Ball: bounce, catch, throw, drop
Swimming pool: float, dive

Extend your vocabulary (Workbook page 40)

> ➡ **Workbook page 40**

Exploring the topic

Aims
Present *will* for predictions about the future
Read about space tourism
Review action verbs

Reading

 Audio CD 2 track 27

Cultural note

* Space tourism is currently only available to very rich people. At the moment, the Russian space program offers trips into space for $20 million. It is fully booked until 2009. Dennis Tito is an America multimillionaire who became the first space tourist. In 2001, he spent almost eight days in space.

Warm-up

Books closed. Ask students where we will go on vacation in the future. Ask them if they would like to go on holiday in space. What is this called? Elicit *space tourism*. Discuss what vacation in space will be like. What things will you do?

1 **General comprehension (first reading); exposure to *will* for predictions**

* Read the sentences.
* Read the text quickly.
* Write the letter of the paragraph next to each sentence.

Answers

1 B	4 E
2 A	5 C
3 D	

2 **Detailed comprehension (second reading); further exposure to *will* for predictions**

* Read the statements.
* Read and listen to the text.
* Choose the correct answers.

Answers

1 T	4 T
2 F	5 F
3 T	6 T

Grammar

1 Grammar chart: *will / won't* (affirmative / negative)

Note:
- We form affirmative / negative sentences with subject + *will / won't* + infinitive (without *to*).
- *Will* is the same for all subjects, e.g. *He will be rich*. NOT *He wills be rich.*
- *Won't* = *will not*.
- We use *will / won't* to make predictions about the future.
- See Grammar summary page 117.

2 Controlled practice of *will / won't*

- Read the jumbled sentences.
- Put the words in order and write predictions about the future.

Answers
1 People will go on vacation to space.
2 People will build houses under water.
3 Robots will clean your house.
4 There won't be any pollution.
5 Cars won't drive on the roads.
6 There will be zero gravity soccer.

3 Grammar chart: *will* (yes / no questions and short answers, *wh-* questions)

Note:
- We form *yes / no* questions with *will* by swapping *will* and the subject,
  e.g. *You will go.* ➡ *Will you go?*
- We form *wh- questions* with *will* by putting a *wh-* word in front of the *yes / no* question,
  e.g. *Where will you go?*
- We form short answers with *Yes,* + subject + *will / No,* + subject + *won't.*
- See Grammar summary page 117.

4 Controlled practice of *will* (wh- questions, *yes / no* questions and short answers)

- Read the skeleton questions and the answers.
- Write *wh-* or *yes / no* questions.

Answers
1 What will schools be like in 2050?
2 How will kids go to school?
3 Will students carry school bags with books?
4 Will teachers teach the class?
5 What time will students go to class?

Finished?

Fast finishers can do Puzzle 10A on page 111.

Answers
BUMP
CLIMB
CATCH
THROW
DIVE
Last word: BOUNCE

Over to you!

5 Personalization; oral practice of *will / won't*

- Read the topics.
- Take turns to make future predictions using the topics in the box (see example).
- Respond appropriately with *I agree.* / *I don't agree.*

Extra activity (stronger classes)

Practice of *will* for future predictions

- Find a group of items in the classroom that students know, e.g. *a pen, some paper, a book, a computer*, etc.
- Ask students to "predict" the future of the objects, e.g. a pen – *We will write with it*, a book – *We will read it.*
- In group of three, students write sentences about the "future" of other objects.
- In feedback, groups read their sentences, and the class guesses the object they are talking about.

➡ **Workbook page 41**

➡ **Mixed Ability Worksheets page 20**

Building the topic

Vocabulary

> **Aims**
> Present and practice vocabulary describing planets
> Model *too / not enough*

Cultural note

- **Mars** is the fourth planet from the sun. The Earth is the third. Mars is also known as the "Red Planet" because it looks red from earth. The planet is about half the diameter of the Earth. Scientists believe there is water under the surface of Mars which means there is a possibility of life on the planet.

Warm-up

Books closed. What do students know about Mars. Could humans live on Mars? (see Cultural note).

1 **Presentation of vocabulary set: describing planets; exposure to *too / enough***

- Read the adjectives in the box.
- Read the text.
- Match the adjectives in the box with their opposites 1-5.
- Listen, check and repeat.

🎧 **Answers / Audio CD 2 track 28**

1	safe / dangerous	4	far / close
2	dry / wet	5	stable / unstable
3	cold / warm		

2 **Vocabulary practice; detailed comprehension task (second reading)**

- Read the statements.
- Read and listen to the text again.
- Choose the correct answers.

🎧 **Audio CD 2 track 29**

Answers

1	T	4	F
2	T	5	T
3	F		

Extra activity (all classes)

Further text comprehension

- Write the questions on the board.
1. When will it be possible to send astronauts to Mars?
2. How cold is Mars in winter?
3. What is the weather like?
4. How much water is there?
5. Why is the atmosphere dangerous?
6. How long does it take to get to Mars?
- Students answer the questions.

Answers
1. Scientists think it will be possible in 20 years' time.
2. It can be -133°C.
3. It is icy and there are dust storms.
4. There isn't any water on the surface.
5. Because there isn't any protection from the Sun's UV rays.
6. It takes over 5 months.

Extend your vocabulary (Workbook page 42)

> ➡ **Workbook page 42**

Grammar

1 Grammar chart: *too / not enough*

Note:
- We use *too* + adjective to say that an amount or a quality of something is more than is desirable or acceptable, e.g. *His house is too far.*
- We can express a similar meaning using *not* + adjective + *enough*, e.g. *His house isn't close enough.*
- See Grammar summary page 117.

2 Controlled practice of *too* + adjective / *not* + adjective + *enough*

- Read the sentences.
- Match the sentences with the same meaning.

Answers

1	C	4	A
2	D	5	B
3	E		

3 Controlled practice of *too* + adjective

- Read the adjectives in the box and the sentences.
- Fill in the gaps with *too* + the correct adjective from the box.

Answers

1	too dry	4	too heavy
2	too expensive	5	too cold
3	too difficult		

4 Controlled practice of *not* + adjective + *enough*

- Look at the picture.
- Read the sentences.
- Write sentences with *not enough,* and the adjective in parentheses.

Answers
1 I'm not old enough.
2 I'm not tall enough.
3 I'm not heavy enough.
4 My bike isn't safe enough.
5 My bike isn't fast enough.

5 Further controlled practice of *too / not enough*

- Look at pictures 1–6.
- Complete sentences 1–6 with *too / not enough* and the adjective in brackets.

Answers

1	too small	4	too tall
2	not close enough	5	too heavy
3	not big enough	6	not warm enough

Finished?
Fast finishers can do Puzzle 10B on page 111.

Answers
short
are too big
cap is not big

Over to you!

6 Personalization; oral practice of *too / not enough*

- Think about an event, concert, or party that wasn't very good.
- Take turns to tell the class the reasons (see example).
- Use *too* + adjective, *not* + adjective + *enough*.

➡ **Workbook page 43**

➡ **Mixed Ability Worksheets page 21**

Living English

Aims

Read about predictions for the Earth
Express uncertainty in writing
Write about predictions in your life
Talk about predictions in your life
Pronounce *I* and *I'll* correctly

Reading

 Audio CD 2 track 30

Cultural note

- **Global-warming** describes the increase in the Earth's temperature. In the 20th Century the temperature of the earth rose 0.6°C. The main reasons for this are an increase in greenhouse gases, especially carbon dioxide. These gases collect in a layer around the atmosphere and prevent heat from escaping.

Warm-up

Books closed. Ask students what they think about the future of the earth. What problems do they think we will face in the future?

Before you read

1 Pre-reading task

- Read the statements.
- Write ✓ if you agree with the statement and ✗ if you disagree.
- Compare your answers with the class.

Answers

Students' own answers

Extra activity (stronger classes)

Students give reasons for their answers in exercise 1.

While you read

2 General comprehension (first reading)

- Read the sentences.
- Read the article quickly.
- Write the paragraph A–E next to the correct sentences.

Answers

1	D	4	A
2	E	5	C
3	B		

After you read

3 Detailed comprehension (second reading)

- Read the phrases in the box and the sentences.
- Read the article again.
- Fill in the blanks with the phrases in the box.

Answers

1	join together	4	evaporate
2	get hotter	5	ski
3	fly	6	live on other planets

Writing

Cultural note

• **EMI Records** is one of the biggest record labels in the world. It was formed in 1931.

1 Presentation of writing skill

Read the Writing skills box.

> ### Writing skills: Making predictions
> • We make predictions about the future with *will*.
>   – *I will ...* indicates the speaker is sure that something will happen.
>   – *I will probably ...* indicates the speaker isn't 100% sure that something will happen.
>   – *I don't think I will ...* indicates the speaker isn't 100% sure it won't happen.

2 Practice of writing skill

• Read the text about Matt's future life.
• Find two examples of the expressions in exercise 1.

Possible answers

(I'm sure)
I'll live in ...   I'll have a ...
I'll work for ...   I'll travel to ...
I'll listen to ...

(not so sure)
The apartment will probably be small ...
I don't think I'll get married young.
I'll probably go to surfing and diving.

3 Detailed comprehension of writing model

• Read the text again.
• Fill in the chart with information about Matt's future life.

Answers

Home	in a big city
	in a small apartment
Work	in a record company
Personal life	a girlfriend and go out with friends
Free time activities	surfing and diving

4 Preparation for personalized writing

• Copy the chart in exercise 3.
• Fill in the chart with information about your future life.

5 Personalized writing

• Follow the writing model and use the chart in exercise 4.
• Write about your future life.
• Use *will, will probably, I think I will ...* .

Speaking

1 First listening

• Look at the pictures and read the model dialogs.
• Listen and read.

🎧 **Audio CD 2 track 31**

2 Presentation of pronunciation point

> ### Pronunciation: *I* and *I'll*
> • *I* and *I'll* are pronounced similarly. It can sometimes be difficult to hear the difference. *I* is pronounced /aɪ/ and *I'll* is pronounced /aɪl/.

• Read the example sentences
• Listen and repeat, copying the pronunciation.

🎧 **Audio CD 2 track 32**

3 Pronunciation practice

• Read the sentences.
• Listen and choose the sentence you hear.

🎧 **Answers / Audio CD 2 track 33**

1 I play tennis.
2 I'll work for a record company.
3 I'll travel to different places.

4 Dialog practice

• Practice the model dialogs with another student.
• Change roles and practice again.

5 Dialog personalization and practice

• Look at the words in blue in the model dialog.
• Think about your future.
• Replace the blue words with ideas about your future to make a new dialog.
• Practice the dialog with another student, pronouncing *I'll* correctly.

➡ **Tests page 20**

10 Review

Vocabulary

1
1 throw
2 drop
3 bounce
4 dive
5 bump into
6 float

2
1 dangerous
2 far
3 dry
4 unstable
5 warm

Grammar

1
1 She won't live in a big house.
2 She will work as a singer.
3 She won't live in Australia.
4 She will have a car.
5 She won't be married.
6 She will have a boyfriend.

2
1 Will she live in a big house? No, she won't.
2 Will she work as a singer? Yes, she will.
3 Will she live in Australia? No, she won't.
4 Will she have a car? Yes, she will.
5 Will she be married? No, she won't.
6 Will she have a boyfriend? Yes, she will.

3
1 It isn't warm enough.
2 It is too dark.
3 It is too easy.
4 It isn't close enough.
5 It is too hot.
6 You aren't old enough.

Reading

1
1 T
2 F
3 T
4 F
5 T

11 Plans

Unit summary

Active vocabulary

- TV jobs: acting coach, bodyguard, casting director, dance teacher, hairstylist, makeup artist
- Health problems: blister, cold, headache, pimple, sore finger, sore throat, sprained ankle, sunburn, toothache

Passive vocabulary

- nouns: acne cream, acupuncture, ambulance, appointment, aspirin, audition, bandage, contestant, electronics engineer, massage, plaster, satisfaction, skin lotion, throat lozenge, tire, tissue, transformation,
- verbs: audition, come back, cut, encourage, explain, fix, perform, treat (an illness)
- adjectives: guaranteed

Grammar

- present progressive for future plans
- *will* (offers)

Skills

- Reading about someone changing jobs
- Reading adverts for health and healthy lifestyle consultants
- Listen to people talking about a coming visit
- Accepting and rejecting invitations

Cross-curricular

- citizenship

Values

- health

Introducing the topic

Vocabulary

> **Aims**
> Present and practice TV jobs
> Review jobs

Warm-up

How many TV jobs can students think of? In pairs, give students a minute to think of as many as possible.

1 Presentation of vocabulary set: TV jobs

- Look at the photos.
- Write the correct number next to each TV job.
- Listen, check and repeat.

Answers / Audio CD 2 track 34

1	hairstylist	4	acting coach
2	makeup artist	5	dance teacher
3	stylist	6	bodyguard

Recycling

2 Review of jobs

- Read the list of words.
- Write the corresponding job next to each word.

Answers

1	actor	4	dancer
2	singer	5	soccer player
3	model		

Extend your vocabulary (Workbook page 44)

➡ **Workbook page 44**

Exploring the topic

Reading

 Audio CD 2 track 35

Warm-up
Are there any TV programs on in the students' country about selecting pop stars? What are their names? What happens on the programs? Do students watch them? Have they ever bought a song by any of the winners?

1 **Comprehension (first reading); exposure to present progressive for future plans.**

- Read the sentences.
- Read the text.
- Choose the correct answer.

Answers

1	F	3	T
2	T	4	F

2 **Detailed comprehension (second reading)**

- Read Daniel's diary.
- Read and listen to the text again.
- Fill in the blanks in the diary with the words in the box.

Answers

1	10 a.m.	4	acting coach
2	rock concert	5	1000
3	9 a.m.	6	auditioning

Grammar

Aims

Present and practice present progressive for future appointments and arrangements
Talk about future appointments and arrangements

1 Grammar chart: present progressive for future plans

Note:
- We use the present progressive to talk about events happening right now.
- We can also use the present progressive to talk about future appointments and arrangements, e.g. in diaries.
- See Grammar summary page 117.

2 Controlled practice of present progressive (affirmative and negative)

- Look at Tina's diary.
- Read the sentences.
- Fill in the blanks with the affirmative / negative present progressive of the correct verb.

Answers
1 is meeting, isn't going
2 are going to, is training
3 is teaching
4 aren't going to
5 are going

3 Controlled practice of present progressive (questions)

- Read the dialog.
- Complete the questions in the present progressive with the verbs in parentheses.

Answers
1 Are you meeting
2 Are you going
3 Are you having
4 are we eating
5 Are we meeting
6 When are you coming back

Finished?

Fast finishers can do Puzzle 11A on page 111.

Answers
He's meeting a friend (Marilyn) at the Mall.

Over to you!

4 Personalization; oral practice of present progressive (affirmative, negative and questions)

- Read the list of activities.
- Complete your diary for tomorrow with three activities.
- Take turns to ask and answer questions about your plans for tomorrow (see example).

➡ **Workbook page 45**

➡ **Mixed Ability Worksheets page 22**

Building the topic

Vocabulary

> **Aims**
> Present and practice health problems vocabulary
> Model *will* for offers

Warm-up

Books closed. Mime a health problem to students and ask them to guess what it is e.g. *sore throat*. Ask other students to mime a health problem to the class and write new words on the board.

1 Presentation of vocabulary set: health problems

- Read the words in the box.
- Look at the pictures.
- Complete the sentences 1–8 with the words in the box.
- Listen, check and repeat.

🎧 **Answers / Audio CD 2 track 36**

1	pimple	5	blister
2	sunburn	6	sprained ankle
3	toothache	7	sore throat
4	cold	8	headache

2 Exposure to *will* for offers

- Read the offers
- Write the number of the health problems next to the correct offers.

Answers

a	4	e	8
b	2	f	3
c	1	g	6
d	7	h	5

Extra activity (all classes)

Revision of vocabulary

- Put students in group of three.
- Students take turns to mime a health problem to the other students in their group. They score a point for a correct answer and a minus point for an incorrect answer.
- After two minutes stop the groups. Who has got the most points.

Extend your vocabulary (Workbook page 46)

> ➡ **Workbook page 46**

Grammar

Aims
Present and practice *will* for offers
Make offers

1 Grammar chart: *will* (for offers)

Note:
- We can make offers with *will* (affirmative).
- We usually use *will* when we have made the decision at the time of speaking, e.g. *I'm cold. – I'll close the window.*
- When speaking we contract *I will* to *I'll*.
- See Grammar summary page 117.

2 Exposure to examples of offers
- Read the statements and the offers.
- Match the statements and offers.

Answers

1	B	4	F
2	E	5	C
3	A	6	D

3 Controlled practice of *will* for offers
- Read the phrases in the box.
- Look at the pictures.
- Write sentences with *I'll* and a phrase in the box.

Answers
1 I'll call an ambulance.
2 I'll style it for you.
3 I'll carry it.
4 I'll show you how to do it.
5 I'll cook the dinner.
6 I'll put a bandage on it.

4 Further practice of *will* for offers
- Read the verbs in the box.
- Read the situations.
- Write sentences using *I'll* and the verb in the box.

Language note
- If we do something for someone else, we use *for you*.
- If a verb is followed by a preposition, e.g. *explain* something *to* someone, we use that preposition, e.g. *I'll explain it to you.* NOT ~~I'll explain it for you.~~

Answers
1 I'll explain it to you.
2 I'll fix it for you.
3 I'll wash them for you.
4 I'll teach you.
5 I'll take you.

Finished?
Fast finishers can do Puzzle 11B on page 111.

Answers
tohtra = throat

Over to you!

5 Personalization; oral practice of *will* for offers.
- Think of a problem.
- Take turns to say your problems and make offers with *I'll* (see example).

➡ **Workbook page 47**

➡ **Mixed Ability Worksheets page 23**

Living English

Reading

 Audio CD 2 track 37

Before you read

1 **Pre-reading task**

- Look at the pictures and the advertisements.
- Answer the question.

Answers
1 a magazine

While you read

2 **General comprehension (first reading)**

- Read the sentences.
- Read the advertisements.
- Write the correct number of the advertisements next to the sentences.

Answers

1	2	4	4
2	1	5	2
3	3	6	1

After you read

3 **Personalization**

- Answer the question and give reasons.

Answers
Student's own answers

Extra activity (all classes)

Further reading comprehension

- Write the questions on the board.
  1 What will OnTrack give you?
  2 What does OnTrack guarantee?
  3 What does The MA Clinic promise?
  4 Where is the MA Clinic?
  5 What is Color Consultants Inc.'s website address?
  6 What will Perfecta do for you?
- Students answer the questions.

Answers
1 Monthly menus, cooking tips, a personal trainer and a support group.
2 It guarantees satisfaction.
3 It promises you'll feel good.
4 Selig, California
5 www.colorconsultants.eng
6 They will match you with a teacher and arrange for you to play with others – even in public.

Listening

1 Present listening skill

- Read the listening skills box.

> **Listening skills: Recognizing numbers**
> - Some numbers sound very similar in English, e.g. *sixteen* and *sixty*. Both words have two syllables but the stress on the words is on different syllables, e.g. six<u>teen</u>, <u>six</u>ty.

2 Practice listening skill

- Read the list of times, addresses, dates and prices.
- Listen and choose the number you hear.

🎧 **Answers / Audio CD 2 track 38**

1 3:50	3 January 8th	
2 19 West Street	4 1:14	5 $30

3 Comprehension of listening text (first listening)

- Read the sentences.
- Listen to the conversation and choose the correct words in each sentence.

🎧 **Audio CD 2 Track 39**

June:	Hello.
Danny:	Hi June! It's Danny. When are you coming to Seattle?
June:	I'm coming on the thirteenth.
Danny:	OK. That's February thirteenth ...
June:	Danny! Not February! January!
Danny:	Oh, right. OK. What day of the week is that?
June:	It's a Friday.
Danny:	Great. So what time is your flight arriving?
June:	It's arriving at twelve forty.
Danny:	Twelve forty. Good. What are we doing then?
June:	Well, we're having lunch with Mike at one thirty.
Danny:	OK. That's lunch, Mike, one thirty. Did you speak to Ria?
June:	Yes, we're meeting her at six fifteen. We're going to a dance club.
Danny:	Cool, see you soon!

Answers
1 plane   2 January   3 lunch   4 dance club

4 Comprehension of listening text (second listening)

- Read the diary.
- Listen again. Choose the information you hear.

Answers
1 January 13th   2 12:40   3 1:30   4 6:15

Speaking

1 First listening

- Look at the pictures and read the model dialogs .
- Listen and read.

🎧 **Answers / Audio CD 2 track 40**

2 Presentation of pronunciation point

> **Pronunciation: accepting and rejecting invitations**
> - When we accept invitations our intonation usually goes up at the end of the sentence. When we reject invitations, our intonation usually falls at the end of the sentence.

- Read the example sentences.
- Listen and repeat, copying the intonation.

🎧 **Audio CD 2 track 41**

3 Pronunciation practice

- Listen to the sentences.
- Put ✓ for accepting or ✗ for rejecting
- Listen and repeat.

🎧 **Answers / Audio CD 2 Track 42**

1 ✗   2 ✓   3 ✓   4 ✗   5 ✗   6 ✓

4 Dialog practice

- Practice the model dialogs with another student.
- Change roles and practice again.

5 Dialog personalization and practice

- Look at the words in blue in the model dialog.
- Think of some different invitations and replies.
- Replace the blue words with your ideas to make a new dialog.
- Practice the dialog with another student.

➡ **Tests page 22**

11 Review

Vocabulary

1
1 hairstylist
2 fashion consultant
3 bodyguard
4 acting chaoch
5 make up artist
6 dance teacher

2
1 D
2 E
3 A
4 G
5 B
6 C
7 H
8 F

Grammar

1
1 She isn't going to have breakfast with her manager 9 a.m.
2 She's going to the hairstylist's at 10 a.m.
3 She isn't going to meet her personal trainer at the gym at 11 a.m.
4 She is going to record a new song with Barry at 12 p.m.
5 She isn't going to give an interview with a magazine.
6 She is going to open a new art museum at 2 p.m.

2
1 I'll get you some food.
2 I'll get you an aspirin.
3 I'll call the dentist.
4 I'll change the channel.
5 I'll call the hairstylist.

Study skills

1 Student's own answers

2 Student's own answers

12 Life experiences

Unit summary

Active vocabulary

- Experience verbs: go bungee jumping, dye your hair, have a piercing, have a tattoo, go on a blind date, go parachuting, go skydiving, go snowboarding
- Embarrassing situations: break, bump into, fall asleep, fall over, snore, spill, talk, wear

Passive vocabulary

- nouns: frog, insect, snail
- verbs: bump, snore, spill
- adjectives: tasty
- other: I kind of like it, in between, wear something inside out

Grammar

- present perfect (affirmative / *never*)
- present perfect (*Have you ever ... ?* / short answers)

Skills

- Reading about people's life experiences
- Review of vocabulary and grammar in a board game

Cross-curricular

- Sport

Values

- citizenship

Introducing the topic

Vocabulary

> **Aims**
> Present and practice experience verbs
> Review verb and noun collocations

Warm-up

Books closed. What are the most exciting experiences students have had in their life? What happened? What experiences would students most like to do?

1 Presentation of vocabulary set: experience verbs

- Read the words in the box.
- Look at the pictures.
- Label the pictures with the words in the box.
- Listen, check and repeat.

🎧 **Answers / Audio CD 2 track 43**

1. have a tattoo
2. go on a blind date
3. go parachuting
4. have a piercing
5. dye your hair
6. go snowboarding
7. do bungee jumping
8. go skydiving

Recycling

2 Review verb and noun collocations.

- Read the words in the box.
- Read the chart.
- Write the words under the correct verbs.

Answers

go	play	do
swimming	computer games	judo
skiing	rugby	karate
surfing	the guitar	

Extend your vocabulary (Workbook page 48)

> ➡ **Workbook page 48**

Exploring the topic

> **Aims**
> Read about an unusual experience
> Exposure to *should / shouldn't*

Reading

 Audio CD 2 track 44

Warm-up

Ask students to read the headings in exercise 1. What kind of experience would students most like to have for each heading, e.g. image change – *I'd like to dye my hair*, going places – *I'd like to go to Australia*, etc.

1 **General comprehension (first reading); exposure to present perfect (affirmative)**

- Read the list of headings.
- Read the text quickly.
- Write the correct headings next to the paragraphs.

Answers

1 Image change   4 Going places
2 Weird food   5 Dating
3 Exciting sports

2 **Detailed comprehension (second reading)**

- Read the statements.
- Read and listen to the text.
- Choose the correct answers.

Answers

1 T   5 T
2 F   6 T
3 T   7 F
4 F

Extra activity (all classes)

Personalisation; present perfect practice; review *would like to ...*

- Write the list on the board.
- *have a tattoo / a piercing, dye your hair, go parachuting / skydiving / skiing / snowboarding, go bungee jumping, go to the United States / Africa / England / France / Italy, go on a blind date, eat snails / frogs' legs / insects*
- Ask students which of the experiences they have had.
- Which experiences would they like to have.
- Encourage students to give reasons for their answers.

Grammar

1 Grammar chart: present perfect (affirmative / *never*)

Note:

- We form the present perfect affirmative with subject + *have / has* + past participle.
- We form the present perfect *never* with subject + *have / has* + *never* + past participle.
- We use the present perfect to talk about experiences in our life so far.
- We use the past simple with time phrases in the past and not the present perfect, e.g. *I played tennis yesterday.* NOT ~~I have played tennis yesterday.~~
- See Grammar summary page 117.

Take note!

Present perfect

- Regular past participles are the same as the simple past forms of the verbs, e.g. *walk* (verb) / *walked* (past simple) / *walked* (past participle).
- Irregular past participles do not follow rules and must be learned (see page 120 for a list of irregular verbs).

2 Controlled practice of present perfect (affirmative)

- Read the advice and look at the pictures.
- Choose the correct word in each sentence: *has* or *have*.

Answers
1	has	4	has
2	has	5	have
3	have		

3 Controlled practice of past participles (regular / irregular)

- Read the chart.
- Complete the chart with the past participles of the verbs.

Answers

Regular	Irregular
played	ridden
watched	been / gone
traveled	met

Extra activity (all classes)

Revision of past forms and past participles

- This activity can be done in pairs or as a class.
- The first student says a verb in the infitnitive form, e.g. *take*.
- The second student says a verb in the past simple form, e.g. *took*.
- The first student finally says a verb in the past participle form, e.g. *taken*.
- Students change roles and start again.

4 Further controlled practice of present perfect (affirmative / *never*)

- Look at the pictures.
- Read the sentences.
- Fill in the blanks with *have / has, have never / has never* and the past particples from exercise 3.

Answers

1	has been	4	have traveled
2	hasn't ridden	5	has watched
3	hasn't met	6	haven't played

Finished?

Fast finishers can do Puzzle 12A on page 111

Answers
Carmen = A

Over to you!

5 Personalization; oral practice of present perfect (affirmative / *never*)

- Think of sentences about your experiences.
- Take turns to tell the class about them (see example).

➡ **Workbook page 49**

➡ **Mixed Ability Worksheets page 24**

Building the topic

Vocabulary

Warm-up

Books closed. Tell students about an embarrassing experience you have had. What are the most embarrassing experiences students have had? What happened?

1 Presentation of vocabulary set: activity verbs

- Look at the pictures.
- Read the words in the box.
- Write the correct number of the photos next to the words.
- Listen, check and repeat.

Answers / Audio CD 2 Track 45

a	fall over	e	bump into
b	talk	f	snore
c	spill	g	break
d	fall asleep	h	wear

2 Personalization; vocabulary practice

- Read and listen to the questionnaire.
- Tick your answers for the questions.
- Compare your answers with the class.

Audio CD 2 track 46

Answers
Students' own answers

3 Practice of regular and irregular past participles

- Read the list of verbs and past participles.
- Match the verbs and the past participles.

Answers

1	D	5	B
2	F	6	C
3	E	7	A
4	G		

Extend your vocabulary (Workbook page 50)

➡ **Workbook page 50**

Grammar

Aims

Present and practice present (*Have you ever ... ? /
short answers*)
Questions

1 Grammar chart: present perfect (*Have you
ever ... ? / short answers*)

Note:

- We form questions with the present perfect
  by swapping the subject and *have / has*, e.g.
  He has been to America. ➡ *Has he been to
  America?*
- We form short answers with *Yes* + subject +
  have / has, or *No* + subject + *haven't / hasn't*.
- We use *Have you ever ... ?* to ask about
  experiences in your life until now.
- See Grammar summary page 117.

2 Controlled practice of present perfect (*Have
you ever ... ?*)

- Read the jumbled sentences.
- Put words in order to make questions.

Answers

1 Have you ever spilled food on a person?
2 Has your girlfriend or boyfriend ever snored at
  the movies?
3 Have your friends ever broken something in a
  supermarket?
4 Have you ever cried in public?
5 Have your classmates ever talked loudly in a
  quiet place?
6 Has your friend ever fallen asleep on the bus?

3 Practice of present perfect (short answers)

- Read the questions in exercise 2 again.
- Write your answers to the questions.

Answers

Students' own answers

4 Practice of present practice (*Have you ever ... ? /
short answers*)

- Look at the pictures.
- Complete the questions with the phrases in
  parentheses.
- Write short answers.

Answers

1 Has Sheila ever been snowboarding?
  Yes, she has.
2 Has Sheila ever eaten insects?
  No, she hasn't.
3 Has Jim ever ridden a motorbike?
  Yes, he has.
4 Has Jim even been skiing?
  No, he hasn't.
5 Have Sheila and Jim ever played the guitar?
  Yes, they have.
6 Have Sheila and Jim ever played the piano.
  No, they haven't.

Extra activity (all classes)

Practice *Have you ever ... ? / short answers.*

- Write the following list on the board:
- Find someone who:
  1 has sprained their ankle
  2 has had a piercing, etc.
- Write about ten items in total.
- Students copy the list, walk around the room and
  ask questions, e.g. *Have you ever sprained your
  ankle?*
- If they find a positive answer, they tick (✓) the item.
- When a student has ticked all ten, the activity stops.
- In feedback, find the names of the people who
  have had the experiences.

Finished?

Fast finishers can do Puzzle 12B on page 111.

Answers

Students' own answers

Over to you!

5 Personalization; written and oral practice of
present perfect (*Have you ever ... ? / short
answers*)

- Write four questions using *Have you ever ... ?*
  and verbs from page 97 and 100.
- Take turns to ask and answer in class (see
  example).

➡ **Workbook page 51**

➡ **Mixed Ability Worksheets page 25**

Living English

Review

Preparation

- Play the game in groups of three or four.
- For each group you need: a dice, a different counter for each player (e.g. a coin).

Rules

- Roll the dice to see who goes first.
- The highest number starts and then the next highest is second, etc.
- On the squares there are instructions.
- Follow the instructions. If you are correct, stay on the square. If you are incorrect, you move back two spaces.
- The first player to get to square 25 is the winner.

Possible answers

1 Any three from: *take a tour, camp, follow the rules, buy a ticket, follow the rules, carry your passports, use a credit card, bargain for souvenirs.*
3 I like speaking English. / I love listening to music. / I hate washing up.
4 In my town there are a lot of cinemas. There aren't many Internet cafés.
6 Any three from: *clean (your) room, cut the grass, make (your) bed, make lunch, put away (your things), set the table, take out the garbage, wash the dishes*
7 What time do you get up?
8 She is tall and she has long dark hair. She's wearing jeans and a blue T-shirt.
9 My school is bigger than my house.
11 Any three from: *creative, competitive, sociable, helpful, disorganised, talkative.*
12 Last year, I sprained my ankle on vacation
13 It was sunny / cloudy / hot / cold, etc.
14 Did you watch a film last weekend?
16 I am the tallest person in my class.
17 At my school, we have to go to lessons. We can't eat in class.
18 What were you doing at 7 p.m. last night?

19 Any three from: *blizzard, earthquake, flood, forest fire, hurricane, tornado, tsunami*
20 I was swimming, when I heard a shout.
22 On vacation you should carry your passport. You shouldn't drop litter.
23 On vacation, I'm going to play football on the beach.
24 Have you ever been skiing?

➡ Tests page 24

12 Review

Vocabulary

1
1 go parachuting
2 have a piercing
3 go bungee jumping
4 go snowboarding
5 have a tattoo
6 go skydiving
7 dye your hair
8 go on a blind date

2 break, spill, fall over, talk, wear, bump into, fall asleep, snore

Grammar

1
1 has been
2 haven't played
3 has met
4 haven't won
5 haven't played
6 has written

2
1 Have you ever lied
2 Have you celebrated
3 Have you bought
4 Have you shouted
5 Have you stolen
6 Have you laughed

3 Students' own answers.

Reading

1
1 He's twenty-one.
2 He goes snowboarding and skateboarding.
3 Yes, he has.
4 He has competed in the X-Games and the US Open.
5 He has won six gold medals.

Workbook 2 Answer key

Remember

1
1 G
2 F
3 A
4 I
5 C
6 B
7 E
8 D

2
1 December first
2 March third
3 January fifteenth
4 June thirtieth
5 September twenty-ninth

3
1 angry
2 happy
3 nervous
4 scared
5 tired
6 surprised

4
1 some, any
2 any, some
3 some, any

5
1 me, I
2 She, her
3 We, us
4 They, them

6
1 ~~boots~~ gloves
2 ~~big~~ small
3 ~~jacket~~ T-shirt
4 ~~short~~ long
5 ~~hats~~ sunglasses
6 ~~shorts~~ sneakers

7
1 What are you doing?
2 I am sitting on the beach.
3 Are you having
4 I am drinking
5 Is your sister sitting
6 she is swimming

8
1 My sister doesn't like basketball.
2 Do you live in London?
3 My dad works at the supermarket.
4 I don't go to school on Sundays.
5 My friend plays the guitar.
6 My parents don't like rock music.

Unit 1

Vocabulary

1
1 soccer
2 computer
3 diving
4 painting
5 shopping
6 band
7 acting

running

2
1 Rick
2 Tim
3 Mel
4 Kim
5 Jack
6 Lily
7 Lee
8 Ray

3
1 Snowboarding
2 hiking
3 Rock climbing
4 camping
5 Snorkeling

Grammar

1
1 going
2 sitting
3 practicing
4 reading
5 running
6 giving
7 living
8 looking

2
1 enjoys
2 Playing
3 Do
4 don't
5 riding
6 Does

3
1 Do you like reading
2 love reading
3 Going to the movies
4 Do you like watching
5 Watching TV
6 enjoy playing
7 enjoy listening
8 loves playing
9 Playing the saxophone
10 hates listening

Vocabulary

1
1 traffic
2 noise
3 pollution
4 houses
5 buildings
6 litter
7 open spaces
8 students' own answers

2
1 fence
2 farm
3 wood
4 bridge
5 field
6 river

Grammar

1
Countable: cars, people, bottles, students
Uncountable: traffic, water, litter, money

2
1 many
2 a lot of
3 much
4 much
5 a lot of
6 many

3
1 How many, are there
2 How much, is there
3 How many, are there
4 How many, are there
5 How much, is there

4
1 much
2 many
3 There aren't a lot of people in the movie theater.
4 We don't have a lot of food.
5 There isn't a lot of traffic in our town.

Unit 2

1
1 play
2 read
3 go
4 listen(s)
5 go
6 watch
7 play(s)
8 eat

2
1 C
2 F
3 B
4 A
5 D
6 E

Grammar

1
1 right now
2 usually
3 right now
4 usually
5 usually
6 right now
7 usually
8 right now

2
1 get up
2 is talking
3 works
4 is having
5 doesn't listen
6 you travel
7 are you wearing

3
1 plays
2 plays
3 isn't playing
4 is sunbathing
5 are swimming
6 is listening
7 comes

Vocabulary

1
1 make, bed
2 make lunch
3 take out, garbage
4 clean, room
5 set, table
6 wash, dishes
7 cut, grass
8 put away, clothes

2
1 fix
2 sweep
3 polish
4 dust
5 do the laundry

Grammar

1
1 cut the grass
2 don't
3 doesn't
4 have to
5 Does

2
1 D
2 E
3 A
4 C
5 B

3
1 has to
2 have to
3 don't have to
4 has to
5 doesn't have to
6 have to
7 don't have to
8 have to

Unit 3

1
1 long, curly
2 short, tall
3 straight, wavy
4 tight, loose
5 low, high

2
1 plain
2 flowered
3 striped
4 checked
5 spotted
6 patterned

Grammar

1
1 bigger
2 shorter
3 curlier
4 better
5 hotter
6 sadder

2
1 funnier
2 tighter
3 fatter
4 worse
5 looser
6 easier

3
1 is bigger than London
2 are tighter than my old jeans
3 is easier than Book 2
4 are noisier than my classmates

4
1 Pamela is shorter than José.
2 José's jeans are tighter than Pamela's jeans.
3 Pamela's room is cleaner than José's room.
4 José is slimmer than Pamela.
5 Pamela's hair is longer than José's hair.

Vocabulary

1
1 creative
2 helpful
3 disorganized
4 talkative
5 competitive
6 sociable

2
1 reliable
2 lazy
3 shy
4 hardworking
5 cheerful

Grammar

1
1. more helpful
2. colder
3. more sociable
4. more difficult
5. thicker
6. more energetic
7. more interesting
8. happier

2
1. F
2. T
3. F
4. F
5. T
6. F

3
1. Ken is more competitive than Tony.
2. Sonja is lazier than Ken.
3. Tony is more sociable that Ken.
4. Sonja is slimmer than Tony.
5. Sonja is more creative than Ken.
6. Ken is stronger than Sonja

Unit 4

1
1. hot
2. cold
3. warm
4. rainy
5. icy
6. windy
7. sunny
8. cloudy
9. snowy

2
1. storm, thunder
2. lightning
3. flood
4. power cut

Grammar

1
1. were
2. was
3. weren't
4. was she
5. wasn't
6. was

2
1. was
2. weren't
3. was
4. wasn't
5. were
6. were
7. was
8. wasn't
9. was

3
1. was
2. Was it
3. It was
4. Were there
5. there were
6. there was
7. Were you
8. I wasn't, was

Vocabulary

1
break
fall
sprain
slip
faint
fell
hurt
blister

2
1. a headache
2. a sore throat
3. a cold
4. a temperature
5. a toothache

Grammar

1
1. regular
2. irregular
3. regular
4. irregular
5. regular
6. regular
7. irregular
8. regular
9. irregular
10. irregular

2
1. arrived
2. telephoned
3. dropped
4. visited
5. carried
6. invited

3
1. wrote
2. met
3. had
4. watched
5. cooked
6. bought
7. went

Unit 5

Vocabulary

1
1. guitar
2. keyboard
3. piano
4. drums
5. microphone
6. bass

2
1. loudspeakers
2. backing singers
3. band
4. stage
5. choir
6. orchestra
7. conductor

Grammar

1
1. Yes, she did.
2. No, they didn't.
3. Yes, she did.
4. No, he didn't.
5. Yes, they did.
6. Yes, he did.
7. No, she didn't.

2
1. come to her party, Yes, they did.
2. eat pizza, No, they didn't.
3. Did Paul go to New York? No, they didn't.
4. Did Paul and his parents stay at a beautiful hotel? Yes, they did.
5. Did Daniel's dad play the piano? No, he didn't.

3
1. didn't have a party
2. didn't drink
3. They didn't stay at a friend's house.
4. He didn't like the weather.
5. He didn't have a big party.
6. They didn't watch a movie.

Vocabulary

1
1 grew up
2 started his career
3 signed a contract
4 recorded
5 had a hit record
6 became famous
7 won an award

2
1 graduated
2 went to college
3 passed
4 applied for a job
5 had an interview
6 offered

Grammar

1
1 E
2 C
3 A
4 F
5 B
6 D

2
1 Where did Sarah put her bag?
2 Why did you arrive late?
3 How many exams did you take last year?
4 What did you wear to the party?
5 How did you make this cake?
6 When did Kim go home?

3
1 did she get up
2 did they go
3 did she phone her
4 How did he break it
5 did he cook
6 did he buy

Unit 6

1
1 wide
2 long
3 narrow
4 big
5 crowded
6 tall
7 small
8 deep

2
1 length
2 height
3 weight
4 length, width
5 depth

Grammar

1
1 deepest
2 most helpful
3 laziest
4 the largest
5 saddest
6 cheapest

2
1 the tallest
2 the funniest
3 the oldest
4 the worst
5 the most expensive
6 fattest

3
1 the hottest
2 the widest river
3 the most talkative boy
4 the biggest building
5 the youngest teacher
6 the best club

Vocabulary

1
1 passport
2 ticket
3 camp
4 tour
5 rules
6 litter
7 credit
8 bargain

2
1 tent
2 map
3 compass
4 backpack
5 hiking boots
6 raincoat

Grammar

1
1 have to
2 can't
3 have to
4 can't
5 have to

2
1 don't have to, can
2 don't have to, can
3 can, don't have to
4 can, don't have to

3
1 have to
2 can
3 can't
4 have to
5 don't have to
6 can't
7 can
8 don't have to

Unit 7

Vocabulary

1
1 They're arguing
2 He's hitting his brother
3 She's hiding
4 She's shouting
5 They're fighting

2
1 robber
2 police officer
3 a witness
4 judge

Grammar

1
1 was
2 weren't, were
3 was
4 wasn't, was
5 was
6 were

2
1 was doing
2 weren't doing
3 were listening
4 was watching
5 were playing
6 weren't listening
7 were watching

3
1 wasn't having dinner, was watching
2 wasn't sleeping, was doing
3 She wasn't watching TV. She was reading a magazine
4 They weren't doing their homework. They were having dinner.

Vocabulary

1
1. street corner
2. fire escape
3. police station
4. bank
5. garage
6. apartment

2
1. post office
2. parking lot
3. library
4. apartment building
5. stadium
6. bus station

Grammar

1
1. D
2. E
3. A
4. F
5. B
6. C

2
1. What was she wearing at the party?
2. Why were you running this morning?
3. Where were they going at lunchtime?
4. Was it raining yesterday morning?
5. Were they playing soccer on Saturday?
6. What was he doing at 8:00?

3
1. was she
2. were they
3. were they talking
4. What was he eating
5. Where were they dancing
6. What was she playing
7. Why was Carlos sleeping

Unit 8

Vocabulary

1
1. blizzard
2. huricane
3. forest fire
4. tsunami
5. hailstorm
6. earthquake
7. flood
8. tornado

2
1. calm, rough
2. light, dark
3. dry, wet
4. dangerous, safe

Grammar

1
1. completed action
2. action in progress
3. action in progress
4. completed action
5. completed action
6. action in progress
7. completed action
8. action in progress

2
1. was
2. cooking
3. opened
4. weren't
5. didn't
6. wasn't

3
1. weren't playing, were playing
2. brake her leg, broke her
3. buy a new house, bought a new
4. waiting outside the movie theatre. He was waiting outside a café.
5. weren't eating candy. They were eating
6. Cathy didn't send a postcard. She sent an

Vocabulary

1
1. angrily
2. quickly
3. well
4. hard
5. carefully
6. happily
7. loudly
8. quietly

2
1. funny
2. interesting
3. difficult
4. valuable
5. strange
6. serious

Grammar

1
1. busily
2. beautifully
3. fast
4. lazily
5. strangely
6. easily

2
1. walks slowly
2. work hard
3. swims badly
4. play well
5. learn quickly
6. drives fast

3
1. quietly
2. good
3. happy
4. carefully
5. loud
6. badly
7. heavy
8. angrily

4
1. quickly
2. well
3. carfully
4. loudly
5. hard
6. slowly

Unit 9

1
1 bend, stretch
2 jump, spin, land
3 kick, hit, pass

2
1 goalpost
2 helmet
3 goggles
4 club
5 ball
6 racket
7 net
8 bat

Grammar

1
1 shouldn't, should
2 shouldn't, should
3 shouldn't, should
4 Should, should

2
1 You should go to bed early.
2 People shouldn't drink a lot of coffee.
3 Students should do their homework every evening.
4 You shouldn't eat fast food every day.
5 Children should visit the dentist twice a year.
6 You shouldn't work all the time.

3
1 What should I do, You should visit the optician.
2 What shold he do? He should exercise more.
3 When should we go? You should go in summer.
4 Where should she go?
5 She should go to a youth club.

Vocabulary

1
1 cycling
2 water skiing
3 lacrosse
4 basketball
5 golf
6 horseback riding
7 track
8 karate

2
1 drop
2 miss
3 throw
4 save
5 roll
6 bounce

Grammar

1
1 David
2 Anita and David
3 Anita
4 David
5 Linda and Eric

2
1 What is Anita going to do?
2 What are Anita and David going to do
3 What is David going to buy
4 When are they going to fly home
5 Is Anita going to do karate
6 Are Linda and Eric going to play soccer.

3
1 Are you going to
2 going to
3 going to go
4 Are you going to
5 I'm not
6 are going to
7 are you going to
8 going to
9 We're going to

Unit 10

Vocabulary

1
1 float
2 drop
3 climb
4 bounce
5 bump
6 throw
7 catch
8 dive

2
1 lifting
2 carrying
3 pulling
4 pushing
5 turn

Grammar

1
1 I won't live with my parents.
2 I will buy a house.
3 Sue won't be a student.
4 She will work in the city.
5 I won't ride a bicycle.
6 I will drive a car.
7 My parents won't give me money.
8 I will have a job.

2
1 Where will people go on vacation?
2 How will we travel?
3 What will students wear?
4 Who will build houses?
5 What time will we start school?
6 How many TV channels will there be?
7 What will schools be like?

3
1 will you be
2 I'll be
3 Will you be
4 won't
5 Will you have
6 I'll have
7 Will you have
8 will
9 we'll have
10 They'll be
11 will you live
12 We won't live
13 We'll have
14 There'll be

Vocabulary

1
1 unstable, stable
2 wet, dry
3 far, close
4 cold, warm
5 dangerous, safe

2
1 mountains
2 valleys
3 volcanoes
4 clouds
5 lightning

Grammar

1
1. too difficult
2. not fast enough
3. too hot
4. too young
5. not close enough

2
1. too dangerous
2. too wide
3. too expensive
4. too heavy

3
1. warm enough
2. big enough
3. quiet enough
4. not good enough

4
1. isn't tall enough
2. He is too old.
3. She isn't heavy enough.
4. He's too young.
5. He's too heavy.
6. He's not fast enough.

Unit 11

Vocabulary

1
1. dance
2. coach
3. hairstylist
4. bodyguard
5. artist
6. stylist

Actors

2
1. audience
2. lights
3. microphone
4. camera
5. stage

Grammar

1
1. No, she isn't.
2. Yes, he is.
3. No, they aren't.
4. Yes, she is.
5. Yes, they are.
6. No, he isn't.

2
1. having lunch with Martha, having lunch
2. meeting Maria in the library, meeting her
3. aren't going to a rock concert in the morning, They are going to a rock concert in the afternoon.
4. She isn't seeing the dentist at 10:30. She's seeing the dentist in at 9:30.
5. They aren't going to the movies at 7:00. They are going to the movies at 8:30.

3
1. Are you playing tennis
2. I'm seeing
3. are you seeing
4. are you doing
5. I'm playing soccer
6. I'm going
7. Is Alison going
8. I'm meeting
9. We're going

Vocabulary

1
1. ankle
2. blister
3. headache
4. toothache
5. throat
6. pimple
7. sunburn
8. cold

2
1. doctor
2. ambulance driver
3. paramedic
4. lab technician
5. nurse
6. surgeon

Grammar

1
1. D
2. F
3. A
4. E
5. C
6. B

2
1. We'll push it for you.
2. I'll pick it up.
3. We'll carry it for you.
4. I'll open the door.
5. We'll fix it.

3
1. I'll buy you a ticket.
2. I'll cook
3. I'll make a cake
4. I'll shut the window.
5. I'll take you to the dentist.

Unit 12

Vocabulary

1
1. tattoo
2. piercing
3. dye
4. snowboarding
5. skydiving
6. bungee
7. parachuting
8. blind

2
1. mountain bike
2. speedboat
3. hang glider
4. scooter
5. rowing boat
6. sports car

Grammar

1
1. played
2. painted
3. watched
4. traveled
5. climbed
6. done
7. met
8. rode
9. wrote
10. ate

2
1. have
2. has
3. have
4. has
5. have

3
1 climbed
2 traveled
3 have ridden
4 have never been
5 has never played
6 has eaten

Vocabulary

1
1 fall over
2 spill
3 break
4 bump into
5 talk
6 wear
7 fall asleep
8 snore
Have you ever been to England?

2
1 see
2 feel
3 hear
4 smell
5 taste
6 seen
7 felt
8 heard
9 smelt
10 tasted

3
1 heard
2 seen
3 smelt
4 tasted

Grammar

1
1 Have you ever fallen asleep in class?
2 Has your teacher ever ridden a motorbike?
3 Have your friends ever visited an art gallery?
4 Have your parents ever been snowboarding?
5 Have you every broken a window?
6 Has your dog ever slept on your bed?

2
1 No, she hasn't.
2 Yes, he has.
3 No, they haven't.
4 Yes, she has.
5 Yes, they have.
6 No, he hasn't.

3
1 you ever visited
2 he ever visited
3 he has.
4 Have Carlos and Amanda ever ridden
5 No, they haven't, have ridden a horse.
6 Have you ever played
7 have
8 Has she every played
9 No, she hasn't

Extra reading 1

1
1 dancers
2 doorkeeper
3 heard

2
1 the passage
2 Box 5
3 the dressing room
4 the stage

3 Students' own answers

Extra reading 2

1
1 cyclone
2 uncle
3 cellar
4 dog
5 bed
6 house

2
1 F
2 T
3 F

3 Students' own answers

Extra reading 3

1
1 T
2 F
3 F

2
1 Hull
2 Guinea
3 Turkey
4 Morocco

3 Students' own answers

Extra reading 4

1
1 c
2 d
3 b
4 a

2
1 F
2 T
3 F
4 T

3 Students' own answers